MORAVIANS IN EUROPE AND AMERICA

1415-1865

HIDDEN SEED AND HARVEST

CHESTER S. DAVIS

WACHOVIA HISTORICAL SOCIETY
WINSTON-SALEM, NORTH CAROLINA
2000

Printed by
Goslen Printing Company
2000

ISBN 0-9704493-0-5
© 2000 by Wachovia Historical Society

Front Cover: Left. Home Moravian Church, Winston-Salem, NC.
Courtesy Charles A. Burrus.

Right top. View of Herrnhut.

Bottom. View of Bethlehem, PA.
Courtesy Archives of the Moravian Church,
Southern Province, Winston-Salem, NC.

Cover Design: Jennie Mejan

Chester S. Davis (1915-   )

Printed in the United States of America

FOREWORD

This monograph, about the Unitas Fratrem, the modern Moravian Church, from the martyrdom of Jan Hus in 1415 to colonial America and the early years of our republic, has been called "the best short history" of the Brethren. It first appeared in 1959 under the auspices of the Wachovia Historical Society and was reprinted in 1973. Each chapter by Chester S. Davis, a former director of the Society, appeared in a series of feature articles in the Winston-Salem *Journal* to commemorate the 500th anniversary of the establishment of the Moravian Church. Because the book, originally titled *Hidden Seed and Harvest*, has long been unavailable, the Society, recognizing the need for a new and revised edition, offers this third printing through Davis's gracious permission.

This new edition is issued to commemorate the tercentenary of the birth in 1700 of Nicholaus Ludwig, Count Zinzendorf, the Lutheran nobleman who offered early Brethren, forced from their Moravian and Bohemian homes by the religious Counter Reformation, refuge on his estates in eastern Germany. Because of increasing knowledge of the origins and evolution of the church sheltered by Zinzendorf, the text has been revised and expanded to include more illustrations and a list for suggested reading has been added. The concluding portion of Chapter X, devoted to the music of the church, has been extensively rewritten by Dr. Nola Reed Knouse, director of the Moravian Music Foundation, which will shortly share new quarters with the Moravian Archives (Southern Province) in the Archie K. Davis Center under construction in Winston-Salem, N.C. Dr. Knouse has also compiled a list of easily available recordings of the works of early American Moravian composers she discussed.

The Publications Committee of the Wachovia Historical Society, Flora Ann Bynum, Dr. J. Edwin Hendricks, Mary Jane Smith, Richard Starbuck, and Susan Taylor, Chair, has been responsible for this edition. The first printing was dedicated to Dr. Adelaide Fries, revered and devoted Moravian historian and archivist. It is appropriate that she should again be recognized in particular because her studies and investigations have contributed so much to this monograph.

Preparing material for publication requires the skill, art, and assistance of many people and organizations. Unfortunately it is impossible to recognize everyone involved in putting together this third printing of *Hidden Seed & Harvest*, and what each person did. So the heartfelt thanks of the Wachovia Historical Society are extended to all those who made this edition possible. In particular Mr. Davis must be recognized for his willingness to let it be reissued and for his advice during its preparation. His support has been critical. Illustrations have been reproduced with gracious consent of Old Salem, Inc., the Moravian Archives (Southern Province), the Archives of the Unity (Herrnhut, Germany), and Charles A. Burrus, Jr. Dr. William McCall made available his unpublished paper about the 26th Regimental Band. Photographic images were provided through the generous support of Old Salem, Inc., and the dedication of Jennifer Bean. The personnel of Goslen Printing, Co., especially Mark Goslen, have been helpful and patient beyond thanks. Without the diligence and devotion of Jennie Mejan, executive secretary of the Society, this project could not have come to fruition.

John H. Felts, MD
President
Wachovia Historical Society

CONTENTS

Illustrations will be found following page 27.

1

Jan Hus and the Establishment of the Unitas Fratrum

In the year 1400, when Jan Hus of Bohemia became a Roman Catholic priest, the times were tinder-dry and lightning flickered in men's tempers. In Bohemia and Moravia, in what is now the Czech Republic, people looked to Rome and, one by one, counted out their grievances.

Originally the people of Bohemia had worshipped in the Greek Church, but now the Roman Church had taken over and people had lost rights which they counted important. In the Eastern Church, for example, both the laity and the priests shared the bread and wine of Holy Communion. But under Rome only the priests held the cup to their lips. This denial of the cup caused anger. So did the fact the Roman Church and its many monastic orders held title to fully half the land of Bohemia.

Moreover, the Bohemians resented the many foreigners, most of them Germans, who ruled them from the high places of government.

And the more outspoken among the Bohemians said that it was wrong that they should be made to worship God in the Latin tongue. "Let us, instead, pray to God in our language rather than in the dead words used by the priests."

Worst of all, Rome was corrupt. This was the time - 1409 - of the Great Schism when Pope John XXIII, a venal and dissolute lecher, fought the pretensions of the two anti-popes, Gregory XII and Benedict XIII.

Others before Hus had sensed this same stirring of nationalism, this same vague belief in the right of individuals to worship as they pleased, and had spoken out against Roman corruption. But Hus, a son born of a poor Bohemian family, expressed the discontent more forcefully than others.

From the University of Prague, which he came to head, and from the Chapel of the Holy Innocents of Bethlehem in Prague, where he preached in the Bohemian tongue, Hus argued and pled for reform within the church. When he was ignored he denounced Rome.

First he clashed with his Archbishop. The Archbishop ordered him to cease preaching at the Chapel of Bethlehem, "that nest of heretics," and then, when he preached on, the Archbishop accused the rebellious priest of heresy.

Hus sent an advocate to Rome to plead his case before the Pope. The advocate not only was ignored, but also thrown into a dungeon. He was dismissed from the Church and declared a heretic. In 1412 he became bolder. He openly said that he trusted the individual to read the Bible and to understand and correctly interpret the will of God from the words he read. This heretical idea - an idea that lies at the base of the Protestant Reformation - shocked the world of Rome.

In 1414 Jan Hus was summoned to appear before the Pope in Constance and recant his heresy. Sigismund, King of Hungary and Emperor of the Romans, furnished Hus with a safe conduct, promising that be could travel to Constance, and later, leave that place without harm.

Hus arrived in Constance on November 3, 1414. His safe conduct was waved aside and he was jailed. At his trial Hus was allowed no defense. He was simply ordered to make a choice: recant his heresy and be imprisoned for life in a walled off cell of a Swedish monastery or be burned.

Jan Hus did not recant.

On July 6, 1415, guarded by a thousand men, Jan Hus was led to a stake. Straw and faggots were piled about him and fired. From the growing flames he spoke one final time:

"Christ, thou Son of the living God, have mercy upon me!"

The martyrdom of Jan Hus only intensified the anti-Roman feeling in Bohemia. His followers, who were called the Husites, continued the protests begun by Jan Hus. In 1419 Wenceslaus IV (or Vaclav), the Bohemian king, responding to Roman pressure, ordered the Husite churches closed. On July 30 of that year the Husites struck back at the King's council. Those councilors who escaped the blow did so by nimbly leaping through the windows of the council chamber and their agility gave the event - the "first Prague defenestration" - its name.

Then, for fourteen years, there was war.

In the beginning, under the leadership of John Zizka, the Husites, arming peasants with flails and using weapons much in the manner modern men use tanks, were successful. But the Husites stood against the combined strength of the Roman Church and the armies of the Holy Roman Empire. More than that, the Husites, though they were all Bohemians, were a splintered people. There were among them radical men who sought to break free from Rome. But there were others who sought only changes in the form of the Roman service.

In time Rome successfully split the conservatives from the radicals and turned the one against the other. By 1433 the Husite Wars were ended and Rome remained the one church, or so it seemed.

The Husite Wars were more than merely another bloody incident in history. Although they occurred long before the birth of Martin Luther, they signaled the coming of the Protestant Reformation. All of the ingredients of the Reformation were there save one, and that was the printing press. Had that tool of propaganda been available to the Husites, it is possible that Hus would have accomplished what Luther and Calvin did later.

As it was, the seeds were planted in the words of Hus. From those seeds came the Brethren of Bohemia, the ones we now call the Moravians, and the first of the international Protestant churches.

In the years of the Husite Wars (1419-1433) the defiant Bohemians splintered into small groups.

At one extreme there were the Taborites, a Puritanical people who objected to what they said was the idolatry of the Roman Catholic Church and openly sought religious freedom outside the Roman framework. Their goal, which also was the goal of Martin Luther in the next century, was to restore the primitive purity and simplicity of the Apostolic Church. To accomplish that goal the fanatical Taborites were prepared to work with sword and fire.

At the other extreme were the Calixtines or Utraquists. They held to conservative views and sought only to have Rome restore their ancient right to partake of the cup of wine at the Holy Communion. Since their quarrel with Rome involved only shallow matters of form, they remained within the mother church and, in time, were used by the Church as allies in the destruction of the Taborites.

But there were others than these. There were, for example, bands of men who could neither accept the warlike ways of the Taborites nor the quibbling of the Calixtines. These were the ones who, like Jan Hus, believed in a "heart religion" that expressed itself by doing rather than by dogma.

It was such a group that Gregory, the Patriarch, nephew of the powerful Utraquist Archbishop Rockyzan (or Rokycana) gathered about him in the village of Kunwald near the Castle of Lititz in Bohemia. There in 1457 or 1458, the exact day is not known; these people established a society - not a separate church - which they called "The Brethren of the Law of Christ." The present-day Moravian Church traces its history back to this society.

In time they came to be known by other names - "The Unity of Brethren," "The United Brethren" or *"Unitas Fratrum,"* "The Bohemian

Brethren" and, most often, simply as "The Brethren" - and we know them today as the Moravians.

Like the Taborites, they lived apart in closely knit villages such as Kunwald, where the law lay in the hands of the elders of the society. Like the Taborites, they practiced economic communism. "They had all things common and parted to all men as everyone had need."

But, unlike the Taborites, the Brethren were a gentle people. They lived by the words of the Bible, distrusting theology or the meanings that other men read into the words of the Bible. They felt that where doctrine attempted to say more than the Bible itself said in plain words, that doctrine was misleading and to be avoided. They trusted the defense of their beliefs to their faith rather than to walls and war wagons as the Taborites had done.

The Brethren patterned their ways on the simple life, expressed in day-to-day Christian living, of the Apostles. In the beginning they sought to live like primitive Christians within the ornate framework of the Roman Church.

Catholic Archbishop Rockyzan tolerated the Brethren so long as they did not break clear of the beliefs and the rule of Rome. But their ways, mild as they were when compared to the fierce ways of the Taborites, outraged the Catholic priesthood and even offended the moderate, form-loving Calixtines.

It was swiftly apparent that there was no place for the Brethren within the Roman Church.

In 1467 the Brethren gathered secretly in the night at a place near Lhota in Bohemia. There, with the help of the Waldensian brothers, a society not unlike their own, the Brethren established a separate church by ordaining their own bishops.

Nine were selected and of these nine, three - Matthias of Kunwald, Thomas of Prychelaus and Elias of Kryschenov - were chosen to be bishops of the Brethren by the lot. On three slips of paper the word *est* (meaning "it is he whom the Lord chooses") was written and six other slips were left blank. These slips were then drawn by solemn brothers and the episcopacy of this ancient church was established.

The use of the lot, as we shall see, continued among the Brethren for some three hundred years. Winston-Salem is located where it is because the answer of the lot was yes.

Until the Brethren broke free from Rome and established their own church, they enjoyed an uneasy peace with Archbishop Rockyzan. After 1467 the fist of Rome was raised against them.

To Rockyzan the Brethren said in 1468, "We have separated from you for no trivial reasons, but because we could not possibly find any spiritual food in your Communion, where faith and love are perishing. Hence we have turned away from you to the Gospel."

That deliberate decision placed the Brethren on the same bloody road which led the Taborites to utter destruction less than a generation before. The Brethren of Moravia held to that road far longer than the Taborites, even though they never defended themselves from their enemies with anything but their naked faith.

2

Persecution and the "Hidden Seed"

When the United Brethren established themselves as a separate church in 1467, they promptly felt the wrath of Rome. More than that, they set the stage for one of history's great object lessons, for they proved, often at the price of their lives, the utter impossibility of destroying an idea by force.

Rome had the physical force and the Brethren, the first of the surviving Protestant Churches, had the idea. Rome acted first. In 1468 the Brethren, those "shameless vagabonds," were declared outlaws.

The Bohemian king drove the Brethren from their villages. Kunwald, where the Brethren first had established their society, was abandoned. Families fled into the mountains where the king's men hunted them down like deer.

In this period Jacob Hulava, who was burned to death in the presence of his family, became the first of the Brethren's long line of martyrs. There were others down the years, many of them.

Armed with nothing except their stubborn faith, these gentle people defied Rome with what we would describe today as passive resistance. Despite the persecution, they held to their ways. In the words of an ancient reporter, "They were forced to meet for worship on the mountains and in the recesses of the forest. In winter they walked in single file to the appointed places, through deep snow, the last man dragging after him a rake or a branch of a tree to obliterate their footsteps."

In time the persecution faded away; but then, under prodding from Rome, it would flame again.

In these years the Brethren reluctantly remained outside the established church. At least twice they sent parties throughout Europe to discover if there was anywhere a congregation which they could conscientiously join. At a synod held during the Fifteenth Century they resolved, "That, if God should, anywhere in the world, awake genuine ministers and reformers in the church they would make a common cause with them." But none was found and the persecution sporadically flared and smoldered.

In 1507 the Edict of Saint James was issued against the Brethren. Their meetings were forbidden, their books burned and their churches destroyed; and for twenty years their scattered membership was hunted as animals of the forest were hunted.

Then, as Martin Luther appeared, Rome turned its attentions to this new troublemaker. Luther's Ninety-five Theses, nailed to the door of the Wittenberg Church in 1517, touched off the Protestant Reformation. For a time at least the Roman Church had more on its mind than the stubborn Brethren of Bohemia.

The Brethren, delighted with the reforms sought by this one-time Catholic priest, promptly assured Luther of their support. For a time they appear to have made an effort to exist within the new church that grew from Luther's teachings.

But such a merger never could last. Luther believed that man was saved by faith alone. The Brethren, however, felt that to be meaningful, faith must find expression through day-to-day Christian living. Lutheranism and the United Brethren went separate ways.

By the time of Martin Luther's death the Brethren had some two hundred tightly organized societies in Bohemia, Moravia and Poland. Although there were occasional periods of persecution - and there always was the threat that the Edict of Saint James might again be invoked - the Church of the Brethren grew large and tremendously influential.

Because they wished their children to know the Bible, the Brethren pioneered in public education. When they had established their own printing presses, the Brethren, anxious to avoid the interpretations of the Roman Church, published the Kralitz Bible, which they translated from the original Hebrew and Greek.

The impact these people had on their times is demonstrated by the fact that in the years 1505-1510 sixty books were published in Bohemia and of that number fifty came off presses owned by the Brethren.

But such unruffled times could not last. Rome, hard hurt by the great explosion of the Reformation, prepared to strike back. In 1609, when Catholic King Rudolph of Bohemia granted his people (less than one-tenth of whom were Catholic) religious freedom, the aggressive Catholic order of Jesuits, which held many of the high places in Rudolph's government, began to apply growing pressure on the Protestants.

In 1618, reacting to this pressure, the Protestant leaders rebelled. A year later King Ferdinand II of Bohemia unleashed the terrifying religious hatreds that characterized the Thirty Years War.

In 1620 the Roman Catholic armies smashed the Protestants at the Battle of White Mountain. On June 21, 1621- "the day of blood" -twenty-seven Protestant nobles, perhaps half of them members of the Unity of Brethren, were executed. In some church histories it is reported that these nobles, in the manner of Christ's apostles, held a love feast on the eve of their execution.

In the wars of the Counter Reformation the Holy Roman Empire deliberately set about exterminating Protestantism in Bohemia. The farms, homes, churches and villages of the Brethren were again destroyed. Graves were broken open and the bones scattered across the land. Under the new laws only a Roman Catholic could be a citizen, enter a hospital, marry, hold property or even write a valid will. Protestant nobles were stripped of their property. All Protestants were told that they must either rejoin the Roman Church or leave Bohemia.

The years of 1624-28 came to be known as "the time of dispersion." It is reported in the old books that 36,000 families of the Brethren alone fled from Bohemia to Moravia, Silesia and Poland to escape the wrath of the Romans. When King Ferdinand II came to power there were some three million persons in Bohemia. When he had completed his work among the Protestants there were less than one million. The others were either dead or banished.

In the history of mankind no church had been so completely destroyed. By 1627 all that remained was what Bishop Jon Amos Comenius described as the "hidden seed."

But that seed - call it, if you will, an idea or an ideal - survived the self-righteous vengeance of the all-powerful Catholic Church. Force destroyed a people that at one time numbered in the hundreds of thousands; but the ideals of those people survived in the "hidden seed."

John Amos Comenius became a bishop of the Church of the United Brethren during the last of those days when the Brethren remained a great educational and religious force in Bohemia.

Comenius was an educator and a writer of international reputation. He has been described, with more than a little justification, as "the father of modern education," One of his books, *The Gate of Language Unlocked*, was translated into fifteen different languages. Comenius was known even in the frontier villages of America. There was a time when he was considered for the rectorship of the new Harvard College in the Massachusetts colony.

Comenius was ordained a bishop of the Brethren when this Bohemian Church had spread into Moravia, Silesia and Poland and ranked among the great religious forces of central Europe.

Long before his death, Bishop Comenius saw his church destroyed before his eyes. As his people melted away, fleeing from Bohemia or, in some instances, remaining in their homes to be beaten back into the Roman Church, Comenius worked to plant what he called the "hidden seed."

He wrote, "We certainly ought to take care that ... the foundations of our unity may not be so entirely mined as to make it impossible for our posterity to find them."

At Lititz, where the Brethren were born in March 1457, and at Fulneck, where they stubbornly held to the last of their churches in Bohemia for a bit longer, Comenius urged his people to cherish their ways and to pass them on, father to son, until the evil days were past.

More than that, Comenius worked to preserve the line of succession of the bishops of the Brethren. It was arranged that others, among them his son-in-law Peter Jablonsky, should become bishops. Although Comenius outlived Peter Jablonsky, the episcopacy of the United Brethren remained intact. One of the links in the unbroken chain was Daniel Ernest Jablonsky, grandson of Comenius.

Daniel Jablonsky lived on into the Eighteenth Century. The Moravians of this day claim that their succession of bishops was kept alive by Daniel Jablonsky and passed on to the renewed church in 1735.

But, except for the "hidden seed" which he planted in the hearts of his people, in his writings, and later in the title of his grandson, Comenius saw his church - the first of the international Protestant churches - vanish.

In the years (1624-1628) of dispersion the Brethren, Comenius among them, fled from Bohemia. They went into Poland, Silesia, Moravia, Prussia, Saxony and Upper Lusatia where they sought refuge.

Comenius attempted to establish a headquarters for the church at Lissa in Poland. Failing in that effort he moved on to Holland. He was only one of many - perhaps 80,000, possibly even 100,000 - refugees who fled from Bohemia when their church and their way of life were destroyed.

In the years that followed the dispersion, the Unity of Brethren, as a formal organization, perished. Some of its people accepted the ways of the established church in their new homes without qualms. Others abided by the forms of the Roman Church but continued to pray for the time when they could worship as they wished. Still others, many of them living near the old centers of the Brethren in Fulneck and Lititz, secretly read from their hidden Bohemian Bibles and practiced the old ways as they best remembered them.

Early in the Eighteenth Century, seventy-five years or more after the dispersion, a restless new spirit of religious awakening washed through these areas.

At Fulneck, for example, families like the Neissers and the Nitsch-manns talked again of the "heart religion" of the old times. In yearning for the earlier ways of their fathers these families talked of abandoning their homes and fleeing from Roman Catholic Moravia to some refuge where they could worship in the manner of the ancient Bohemian Brethren.

Christian David, a wandering Moravian carpenter, knew the Neissers and the Nitschmanns and he knew also of their dreams. Being a fellow with an astonishing range of acquaintances, David also just happened to know a young nobleman named Zinzendorf and he recalled that Zinzendorf had at one time expressed an idle interest in locating refugee families on his estate in Saxony.

Comenius had planned for the survival of his church. Yet except for the wandering carpenter Christian David, the plans of Comenius might well have become lost in one of the smaller footnotes of history. As it was, the ancient Church of the Brethren was rediscovered and the "hidden seed" ripened and flowered again. Carpenters have had an astonishingly large place in Christian history.

3

Count Nicolas Zinzendorf and the Flowering of the "Hidden Seed"

Christian David was a man who got things done. If he didn't always do things wisely, he at least carried them out with dispatch.

This itinerant Moravian carpenter, a Roman Catholic by birth and a Lutheran by choice, met Count Nicolas Zinzendorf in Dresden where the young Count was serving as a legal counselor to the King of Saxony.

The fact that a member of the Austrian nobility should entertain a social relationship with a wandering tradesman was highly unusual in the early Eighteenth Century. But then, Zinzendorf and David were most unusual men. Their meeting ground was a common and profound interest in religious matters.

At the time of their meeting in May 1722, David told Zinzendorf of the Moravian families who yearned for some place of refuge where they could practice the "heart religion" of the primitive Christians. Zinzendorf, who only the month before had purchased an estate at Berthelsdorf in Upper Lusatia, said that he would consider settling a few such families on his land.

Presumably while the Count was considering this proposition, David acted and, thereby, made up the Count's mind. The wandering carpenter hustled off to Moravia, sought out the Neisser family and told them of the "offer" made by Count Zinzendorf. On May 25, 1722, David led the Neisser party - there were ten in all - out of Moravia and on to Berthelsdorf where they arrived on the eighth of June.

The Count was absent at the time and his grandmother, a bit flabbergasted at David's story, allowed the Neissers to take up some unoccupied land located at the foot of the *hutberg* (watch hill) on the road that ran from Lubau to Zittau.

This place they called Herrnhut (meaning "Under the Care of the Lord" or "Standing Guard for the Lord") and on June 17, 1722, Christian

David felled the first tree. As his axe bit into that tree David quoted, "Here hath the sparrow found an house, and the swallow a nest for himself."

The suddenness of David's action astonished Zinzendorf when he returned to his estate and discovered that he had unexpected guests. But at that time the Count was not acquainted with the unexpected ways of Christian David. Many years later he was to say of that curious man, "There was only one."

Once the flow of emigrants from Moravia began it was zealously encouraged by David.

He made periodic trips into Moravia to interest others in joining the new society. Proselyting of this sort was hazardous. Only a few years later David Nitschmann, the Martyr, was arrested while on a similar errand in Austria. He was imprisoned and he died in prison.

On May 2, 1724, Christian David guided "the five young men of Zauchtenthal" - the three David Nitschmanns (*i.e.*, the Martyr, the Bishop, and the Weaver), Melchoir Zeisberger, and John Toltschig - to Herrnhut. These men, all of them from prosperous families, risked much in fleeing. Yet, they were among the few who had stubbornly held to the dimly recalled ways of the ancient Brethren of Bohemia. They were a part of the "hidden seed" planted so carefully by John Amos Comenius.

By 1727 there were about three hundred refugees in Herrnhut. Since most of these people had come from across the mountains in Moravia, their neighbors described them simply as "the Moravians."

The Herrnhutters were a mixed lot. Their religious backgrounds ranged from Roman Catholic to Lutheran and included a variety of dissenters. Along with Moravians there were Poles, Germans and Bohemians. There were fanatics among them and bigots fleeing from bigotry. Clash and friction, of course, were inevitable.

By 1727 the village was split into at least three camps.

1. There were those who wished to join the Lutheran Church.

2. There were others - and this group included Zinzendorf - who wished to develop a Christian society within the general framework of the Lutheran Church.

3. Still others wished to re-establish a church patterned on the simple ways of the primitive Christians. The Nitschmanns and many of the migrants from Moravia favored this course.

For a period of some weeks Zinzendorf lived among the Herrnhutters, talking with them, and determining just what it was they wished. Undoubtedly he learned something of the ancient Unity of Brethren from men like the Nitschmanns. At some point during 1727, Zinzendorf rediscovered in the writings of Comenius the discipline -the Rules and Regulations - of the Bohemian Brethren.

On May 12, 1727- Zinzendorf called it "the critical day" - the Count assembled the villagers before him at "the great house" and read aloud his "Brotherly Agreement of the Brethren from Bohemia and Moravia and others, bidding them to walk according to the Apostolic rule."

These rules - and they ranged from the use of strong drink to the care of children and the responsibility for the aged - were, in effect, the constitution and bylaws of the way of life Zinzendorf wished to establish at Herrnhut. The brotherly agreement appealed to the villagers. Perhaps because it sought to blueprint a simple, Christian way of life, the agreement was remarkably similar to the disciplines of the Church of the Bohemian Brethren. Certainly the strongest link between the church of the Fifteenth Century and Herrnhut was the emphasis on day-to-day Christian living.

May 12, 1727, and August 13, 1727 (a day when, during a period of religious exaltation, the villagers felt the spirit of God come among them), are days from which the Moravian Church dates the renewal of the ancient Church of the *Unitas Fratrum.*

Actually Zinzendorf had no intention of creating a separate church. What he had done - or so, at least, he thought - was to effect a compromise. His agreement with the villagers (1) required that they remain members of the parish Lutheran Church at Berthelsdorf but (2) allowed them to manage their spiritual affairs as a distinct Christian society within the Lutheran Church as it existed at that time.

Yet, even in 1727 Count Zinzendorf must have appreciated the difficulties of such a compromise. That problem was to plague him for life.

In the early Eighteenth Century it was unthinkable that a member of the nobility should make a vocation of religion. The nobility was born to rule. Count Nicolas Zinzendorf, however, managed to· have his cake and eat it too. He made a vocation of religion and he ruled as long as he lived.

As Brother Zinzendorf he reported, "I can say with truth that my heart was religiously inclined as far back as I can recollect." That abiding and genuine inclination lasted as long as Zinzendorf drew breath.

But, as Count Zinzendorf, he confessed, "I was not free from pride with reference to my rank as one of the nobility. It did not carry over into things pertaining to the affairs of Christ."

Since the Moravians were dedicated to the day-by-day living of a determined Christian life, in which the spiritual and the secular intermixed in a manner which often made the one indistinguishable from the other, their society provided Zinzendorf with a unique opportunity to wear both his hats without undue embarrassment.

The Count was well educated, studying both at the University of Halle and the University of Wittenberg and earning the respect of scholars at each place. At Halle, where his unusual absorption in religious matters was considered unbecoming in a young nobleman, Zinzendorf was, from time to time, charged with a variety of misdemeanors which included lying, disobedience, vanity, hypocrisy and trouble making.

Later, at the University of Wittenberg, where he studied law, accounts of his behavior were less critical - perhaps because Zinzendorf had by that time stubbornly won his right to follow his spiritual interests as he saw fit.

While still a student he established "The Order of the Grain of Mustard Seed," a religious society whose members wore rings inscribed, "No one livith unto himself." The members of the order pledged three things:

To be kind to all men.

To be true to Christ.

To send the Gospel to the heathen.

Zinzendorf remained true to those pledges. The spirit of the first two caused him to allow the Moravian refugees to settle on his estate in Saxony and build their village of Herrnhut. The third pledge resulted in the Moravian Church becoming the mother of the Protestant mission movement.

Nicholas Zinzendorf was born on May 26, 1700. Except for a very brief period (1722-1727), when he served as a legal counselor of the King of Saxony, he devoted his adult life and his fortune to the Moravians. By the time of his death in May 1760, Zinzendorf had forever impressed the print of his character on the Moravian Church.

Zinzendorf was a strange and contradictory man. His mind was quick and he possessed an amazingly retentive memory. Because of his noble birth, doors opened readily to him. And because of his personality, warm and attractive if sometimes a bit pompous, those doors generally remained open.

He was a gifted speaker and, perhaps, even more talented as a writer. That was particularly true of verse, where he found that words poured into his mind faster than his pen could capture them on paper. Zinzendorf ranks among the most prolific of the Protestant hymn composers. Like the members of the early Bohemian Brethren he believed in the power of words and made diligent use of the printing press.

Unlike many religious leaders Zinzendorf respected the beliefs of other churches. To the end of his life he remained a devout Lutheran. Yet, he also admired many adherents to the Roman Catholic faith. The fact he, a Lutheran minister, was ordained a Moravian bishop by a member of the Reformed Church is typical of his tolerance.

Even so, the Count was a man who was born to rule. When others challenged his ways and his beliefs - and the theologians of his time often did just that - sparks flew. John Wesley, the founder of Methodism, at one point in his life was genuinely attracted to the Moravians and might have joined with them had he been able to accept what he felt were the domineering ways of the Count.

From the time the Moravians first came to Herrnhut until the time of his death, Zinzendorf stubbornly refused to acknowledge that the Brothers were members of a separate church. To him they were never more than members of a Christian society who practiced their way of life within the framework of the established church: the little lump of leaven that leaveneth the entire loaf.

This diaspora concept - the Count liked to talk of the small church within the larger church - explains why the Moravians, unlike the other Protestant groups, never grew to be large-sized. They sought no members. Even in their missionary work they did not seek converts for their church. Instead, they brought the message of the brotherhood of man through Christ, converted the heathen, and then encouraged those converts to become members of an established church.

But even in advocating the diaspora concept, Zinzendorf often preached better than he practiced. For time and again, while he talked of a church within a church, Zinzendorf led the Moravians into steps which could only result in creating a separate church. He did that, for example, when he re-established the ancient line of succession of the Moravian bishops in 1735.

In dealing with the heathen, Zinzendorf preached that the missionaries should never lord it over the natives. Yet, in his three visits among the Indian tribes on the Pennsylvania frontier, Zinzendorf's nose crinkled in disgust and he carefully pitched his tent well to the side of the main Indian camps.

In church management the Count talked much of economy. Yet he handled his own finances in a manner that came close to wrecking the Moravians and landing a goodly part of their leadership, Zinzendorf included, in a debtors' prison.

At another time - and just when the Moravian Church was beginning to prosper nicely - Zinzendorf became "Little Papa" to his flock of "lambkins" and led the church through a swamp of treacle that nearly suffocated the Moravians in mawkish sentimentality.

In the Moravian towns the importance of the family and of the raising of children was emphasized by Zinzendorf. It was a point he stressed in the Articles of Brotherly Agreement in 1727.

Yet the Count blithely left his wife to bear his children and shoulder his tangled financial affairs while he wandered far and wide in the company of Sister Anna Nitschmann.

Those contradictory characteristics are important only in that they help to spotlight some of the contradictions within the Moravian Church itself. For the modern Moravian Church is at least as much a product of Zinzendorf's personality as it is a continuation of the ancient ways of the Brethren of Bohemia.

Zinzendorf alone made it possible for the Moravian Church to become what it is today. But - and this is the frustrating, contradictory part of the Moravian story - because of Zinzendorf the Moravian Church did not become more than it is today: a small, little-known body possessing an immensely rich and ancient history.

4

Herrnhut and the Developing Pattern of the Moravian Church

The pattern for the development of more than twenty Moravian settlements all around the world was cut at Herrnhut in the years immediately after the adoption of the Brotherly Agreement in 1727.

In order to weed out possible troublemakers and those who were weak in faith, the Brothers screened all persons who sought to join their Herrnhut society. Once newcomers were accepted they abided by the laws of the village or they were asked to leave.

It is a mistake to believe that life in Herrnhut was placid and unruffled after 1727. There still were occasions of discord and friction. But after 1727 the villagers were organized and capable of handling their problems as they arose.

At Herrnhut the elders of the church watched over every phase of life, both spiritual and secular. The village operated on a communal basis in which each member contributed according to his ability and shared according to his need. It was, in the economic although not in the Marxist sense, a communistic society modeled on the ways of primitive Christians.

Over the past two and a half centuries there have been hundreds of experiments in communal living. Most of them failed swiftly. But the Moravians, with their peculiarly rigid and yet flexible organization, were surprisingly successful.

Through the choir system - a system in which the villagers were divided into groups according to age, sex, and marital status - the church elders not only kept an eye on village affairs, but also watched the behavior of each individual member.

Another reason for the success of the Moravian communal villages lies in the fact the Moravians lived in a hostile world. In Europe there was the threat of religious persecution. Later, in America there were the Indians.

These forces tended to accentuate the already introspective ways of the Moravians. They lived apart by choice, but, in part, it was the choice of their neighbors who suspected that the Brethren were up to no good.

At Herrnhut, for example, the Moravians were suspect for many reasons:

1. The continued illegal emigration out of Moravia and Bohemia angered the ruling powers of those lands. Although a good part of these emigrants went to other places than Herrnhut, Zinzendorf regularly was blamed.

2. The absence of class distinctions at Herrnhut smacked of subversion. So did the fact that Zinzendorf, a nobleman, made a vocation of religion and a fetish of democratic action.

3. There were endless rumors of the barbaric customs of the Moravians. At one time, for example, it was said that the Brothers went into their graveyard on Easter morning, opened the graves, and wakened the dead with trumpets.

4. The Roman Catholics distrusted the freedom the Moravians allowed their lay members. Protestants, on their part, were suspicious of Zinzendorf's friendship with Catholic leaders.

But worst of all was the fact that while Zinzendorf sincerely tried to keep the Moravians as a Christian society living within the Lutheran Church, the Lutherans themselves never were able to absorb these strange people. As a result, Lutheran leaders came to consider the Moravians as separatists.

In 1732 and again in 1736 the Lutheran Church sent delegations to Herrnhut to investigate the Moravians. In both instances the Brethren were given clean bills of health and even faintly praised for their ways. But in 1736 Count Zinzendorf was banished from Saxony; his period of exile lasted ten full years.

During his years of exile Zinzendorf established a footloose band which he called "the Church of the Pilgrims," and he also established a second Moravian center, called Herrnhaag, in Wetteravia. Within an amazingly short time Herrnhaag grew to be larger than Herrnhut.

In these same years the Moravians, then just launching their mission program, felt a growing need of a ministry of their own. Zinzendorf recognized that he could not always depend on the Lutheran Church to supply him with men of a sort who would work well within the tight-knit Moravian society. He, therefore, created a separate Moravian ministry.

In 1735 two bishops of the Church of the ancient Brethren of Bohemia still lived, Daniel Ernest Jablonsky (grandson of John Amos Comenius) and Christian Sitkovius of the United Reform and Brethren Church of Poland. On March 13, 1735, Jablonsky, with the written approval of Sitkovius, ordained David Nitschmann, the carpenter, the first bishop of the renewed church.

In 1737 Zinzendorf, then a Lutheran minister, also became a Moravian bishop.

In this same period Zinzendorf established a seminary at Herrnhaag and the Moravians began to train their own ministers.

Both these steps - the revival of the episcopacy of the ancient Unity of Brethren and the establishing of a Moravian seminary - plainly violated Zinzendorf's repeated statements that the Moravians were simply a small Christian society operating within the Lutheran Church. Although Zinzendorf never would admit it, his own deliberate actions supplied legitimate ammunition to critics who called the Moravians separatists.

By 1735 the Moravian Church was incandescent.

Individual brothers and small bands wandered about Europe spreading the word of their way of life. They were not evangelists, for they did not preach, but, rather, traveling messengers. They spread seeds from which new Moravian societies sprang in places as far away as Holland, England, and Denmark.

By 1735 this handful of people had launched the most ambitious mission program the Protestant world had ever known. More than that, they had begun their settlements in America.

Even though Herrnhut itself was less than fifteen years old the customs of the Moravian Church already had taken form by 1735. In part, that was because the Brethren drew their ways from deep in the past. And, in part, it was the result of Zinzendorf's tendency to invent and then quickly make a tradition of his inventions.

In the Moravian Church the emphasis was on Christian living rather than Christian doctrine. Day by day, from birth to death, the Moravians sincerely tried to make religion as much a part of their life as breathing.

Christ's apostles provided them with their pattern. On that score the German philosopher Goethe observed, . . . it is delightful to go back to the time of the Apostles, where all stands forth as fresh and immediately spiritual. The Moravian doctrine had something magical in that it appeared to continue, or rather perpetuate, the conditions of those first times."

John Wesley, the father of the Methodist Church, came to know the Moravians well in Georgia. He said, "They were always employed, always cheerful themselves and in good humor with one another." After visiting in Herrnhut, Wesley added, "I would gladly have spent my life here…"

Because of their preoccupation with their own way of life the Moravians avoided politics. They refused to take oaths and until 1831 they refused to bear arms. "It does not accord with our character as Brethren," they said, "to mix in such political affairs. We are children of peace and wish peace of all men; whatever God lays upon us, that we will bear."

While the Moravian Church is presbyterial in the sense it is governed by elders, the church has no one leader. Until 1741 the Moravians had a chief elder. Since then, however, they have left that position vacant and looked upon Christ as their chief elder.

The characteristic of fellowship in Moravian worship is, perhaps, best illustrated by the love feast. Here the members of the congregation come together to share food and drink (today buns and coffee) in the manner of the common meal of the primitive Christians. The love feast reflects Zinzendorf's statement, "I acknowledge no Christianity without fellowship."

Some of the church historians trace the love feast back to the times of the Husites. Others see the love feast as a practice reflecting the fellowship of the apostles. But, whatever its source, this practice developed at Herrnhut when Zinzendorf invited the villagers to "the great house" to celebrate some such social occasion as a wedding. Certainly love feasts were an established part of the church ritual at Herrnhut. They remain a warm part of the present church. The Candlelight Love Feast on Christmas Eve somehow is capable of causing tears to moisten even a cynical eye in this skeptical day.

The Moravian Easter sunrise service also began at Herrnhut, where, in 1732, a band of the Single Brothers climbed the "watch hill" or *hutberg* to welcome the dawn of Easter Day with songs and prayer. The first sunrise service in North Carolina was held on God's Acre -the burial place of the equal dead - at Bethabara in 1758.

Easter, marked by the hopeful cry "The Lord is risen!" remains the greatest of the Moravian Church celebrations. On God's Acre, where the bodies of the dead are sown in choirs and marked by simple stones, all of a size and all lying flat on the ground, the Moravians gather to this day to greet the Easter dawn with prayer and the music of massed bands.

The Moravian daily text traces back to 1728 when Zinzendorf selected a verse from the Bible as a reading for each day. The text was read in the morning on the day for which it served as the "watchword." Until 1731 the daily text was selected the evening before the day on which it was to be used as the "watchword." Since 1731 the daily text has been prepared a year in advance and printed in book form. Zinzendorf was writing the texts for 1761 at the time of his death.

Now that the *Singstunde* (song service) is no longer a regular part of the worship service, Moravian families gather at their tables for the evening meal and bow their heads while the watchword of the day is read aloud.

In all of their settlements the history-loving Moravians maintained day-to-day diaries. Each day they jotted down the events of that day and no event was so trivial that it escaped notice. With the Moravians the fall of a sparrow was not only noted; it was recorded.

These diaries - in North Carolina they run back to 1752- and the Memorabilia, in which on New Year's Eve the minister of the congregation sums up the events of the preceding year, are immensely valuable historical documents. The threads of Winston-Salem's past that dangle down into this day are available to us primarily because the Moravians rank among the world's foremost historical string-savers.

Because they were both an international and a highly literate church, their leaders maintained a worldwide interchange of letters, reports, newspapers (including the *Wochen*, a church publication), books, pamphlets and the like. In the early days, when the Moravian villages were scattered across four or five continents, the Brethren gathered to hear the mail read aloud. In time, this custom developed into a monthly Unity Day.

The Cup of Covenant service in the Brethren pass the cup one to another in solemn ceremony of covenant and commitment was begun in Herrnhut in 1729.

Many of the old customs, of course, have vanished. Perhaps the most interesting among these is the lot.

While the use of the lot was not peculiar to the Moravians - it was used by most Pietist groups in the Eighteenth Century - it does have a peculiarly ancient history among the Brethren. The Bohemian Brethren, from whom the present church springs, used the lot in the Fifteenth Century to select their first bishops.

The lot was never, or, at least, very rarely, used frivolously. On that score the Moravians said, "No one must use the Lot unless his faith is strong, nor unless there is a need. In using it a man must not feel: 'Dear Saviour, I hope you will feel as I do,' but must be in such a frame of mind that with his whole heart he can say, 'Dear Saviour, I have nothing, I make no choice, show me Thy will and I will be Obedient thereto.'"

In using the lot there were, most often, three choices; *"Yea," "Nay"* and a blank. Care was spent in preparing a question for the lot. Only the church elders could put a question to the lot.

There is a kinship between the lot as the Moravians used it and the flip of a present day coin. But there is a difference too.

The Moravians first studied a problem. In the case of locating the site where they planned to build Salem they checked the central parts of the Wachovia tract thoroughly. As a result of this investigation they selected several possible sites. They then picked the site where this city now stands through the drawing of lots.

As they used it, the lot was a sign of humbleness. Through their use of the lot the Moravians, in effect, said, "Lord, I have pondered over this problem and I have not yet discovered the answer. In Your infinite wisdom help me."

One of the clearest measures of the strength of the Moravian faith is found in the fact they accepted the answer of the lot. In some cases - as, for example, where a Single Brother sought to marry a Single Sister and the lot said "No" - the answers were hard to accept.

5

The First International Protestant Church Comes to America

The description of Christian mission work found in the cynical verse "First they fell upon their knees and then upon the aborigines" undoubtedly would have horrified Count Nicolas Zinzendorf.

From his university days, when he organized "The Order of the Grain of Mustard Seed" and pledged himself to carry the word of Christ among the heathen, Zinzendorf was driven by a restless urge to establish missions in far-off lands.

Whether he deliberately shaped his Moravian brotherhood for that purpose is not certain. But it is significant that the Moravian congregation was ideally adapted to mission work. No group, unless it was the bachelors of the Roman Catholic priesthood, was better organized for that purpose.

In 1727 the congregation at Herrnhut was divided into small bands according to age, sex and marital status. This developed into the Moravian choir system. There were ten choirs: the Married Choir, the Widowers, the Widows, the Single Brothers, and the Single Sisters, the Youths, the Big Girls, the Little Boys, the Little Girls and the Infants in Arms.

The administrative machinery within the more important choirs -the Single Brothers and Single Sisters Choirs, for example - was almost a duplicate of the administrative machinery of the village itself.

Because of the choir system - the Moravians considered it a troop system in a peaceful army led by Jesus Christ - individuals had great freedom of action. Married Brothers and Sisters, for instance, could leave Herrnhut and travel half around the world on a mission assignment with an easy mind for they knew that their family would be well cared for within the choir system.

The opportunity to lead his army into the mission field came in 1731 when, as a result of a visit to the Danish court, Zinzendorf met a West Indian slave named Anthony Ulrich. The Negro told the Count of the spiritual destitution that existed among the slaves in the West Indies. Ulrich later traveled to Herrnhut and repeated his story to the full congregation.

Two Single Brothers, Leonard Dober and Tobias Leopold, volunteered to go to the West Indies, as missionaries. When the lot was consulted Leopold drew a "No." Dober, however, persisted and, despite some opposition from Brethren who feared such a risky venture into the unknown, the lot was again consulted. This time the answer was, "Let the youth go, for the Lord is with him."

Dober made the trip to Saint Thomas in the West Indies in late 1732 with David Nitschmann, then known as the Carpenter. He had not yet become the first bishop of the renewed church.

The early Moravian missions were peculiar in that they rarely received financial support from home. Zinzendorf, making a virtue of the fact the church had no money, insisted that the missionaries make their own way in whatever land they worked. In Saint Thomas, where the economy was based on Negro slavery, this was not easy. But Dober, Nitschmann (who hammered and sawed), and the brothers and sisters who came later somehow managed to finance their mission program. It was the same elsewhere.

Although the Moravians carefully avoided becoming entangled in secular matters - in the touchy master-slave relationship, for example - there was trouble. When Zinzendorf visited the West Indies in 1739 he found his missionaries in jail. They had been called as witnesses in a theft case and they appeared. But, in the Moravian custom, they refused to take an oath. The judge threw the stubborn fellows into the local jail.

In the West Indies the Moravians converted 13,000 Negro slaves before another Protestant Church established a mission in the islands.

In 1733 three men (one of them that amazing carpenter, Christian David) traveled to Greenland and established a mission among the Eskimos. Here again there was trouble in the beginning, most of it native hostility triggered by an outbreak of smallpox. The first convert - a man named Kajarnak - was not enlisted until 1738. However, by 1758 the Moravians had baptized about four hundred Eskimos.

In 1734 the Moravians attempted to establish a mission among the Swedish Laplanders. When it was discovered that another church was working that field the Moravians retired. An effort was made to shift this project to Siberia but it was blocked by the suspicious Russian government.

By 1735 the Brethren had a mission in Surinam (Dutch Guiana), where the climate, the snakes, the Indians, bands of escaped slaves and some internal discord made conditions impossible. "It often happened that a missionary could be well in the morning and in the grave by night time."

In Surinam every convert was gained at the cost of a missionary's life. The Surinam project was abandoned in 1745 but the stubborn Moravians reopened the mission in 1754. This time it survived.

In 1752 an effort (which cost six lives) was made to place a mission in Labrador. That effort failed. But, here again, the Brethren persevered and a mission was opened in Labrador in 1771.

The Moravians established missions in Ceylon, among the Hottentots of South Africa, in Cairo, Jerusalem, Constantinople, Bagdad, and among the Indians of North America. They had the first mission among the lepers and the first Protestant mission among the West Indian slaves.

Zinzendorf was careful in the selection of brothers and sisters for mission work. Before he approved of Dober's venture into the West Indies he took the young man on a long journey in order to study his character and capabilities. Once selected, these mission workers were painstakingly trained for their assignment.

The Count's rules for mission work were simple and effective. He required that the Moravian missions be self-supporting. He insisted that the missionaries live among the natives and avoid lording it over the heathen." He warned them not to attempt to convert an entire people but, instead, to concentrate on individuals. And, in the spirit of the Moravian Church, he told them to stick to the Gospel and avoid theology.

Because Zinzendorf always believed that one day the Moravian Brotherhood would be absorbed by other churches, the Moravian missionaries made little effort to gain members for their church. In the West Indies, for example, Brother Frederick Martin won seven hundred converts in 1736. Yet, of these, he baptized only thirty.

The Moravians carried the cross of Protestant Christianity across the world, establishing missions in places as far scattered as the Cape of Good Hope and Greenland. They did that despite the fact they were few in number and penniless. They did it because they believed, because they believed with an incandescent faith that is rarely found among any people.

The fantastic truth is that these Moravians - and in 1731 there were no more than a handful of them - built the foundations of the present day Protestant mission movement.

In 1732, when the Moravians began their foreign mission program, Count Zinzendorf had other problems than the heathen to ruffle his mind. Herrnhut, long suspected as being a harboring place of separatists, was under attack. Zinzendorf recognized the necessity of decentralizing the Brotherhood.

The mission program offered one step in that direction. Another step was to establish new Moravian centers, like Herrnhaag, in Europe. America offered another and more promising opportunity. In the New

World the possibilities of mission work among the Indians made the prospects doubly attractive.

In 1734 the Moravians obtained a grant of land (including two town lots in the present city of Savannah) in the colony of Georgia. In April of 1735 August Gottlieb Spangenberg - known to the Brethren simply as "Brother Joseph" - led a party to the new land.

In the following year Bishop David Nitschmann guided a second party to Georgia. This group made the long sea voyage with John and Charles Wesley.

By 1740 the Georgia settlers had cleared themselves of debt, paying for both their land and for the costs of their voyage. But, at that same time, war between England and Spain broke out. Georgia, caught between the English Carolinas and Spanish Florida, became a battleground.

The Moravians, rather than abandon their conscientious objections to bearing arms, abandoned instead the gains they had won at such great effort in Georgia. They turned their backs on what they had built and started north toward the Pennsylvania colony.

The Georgia venture was not an entire loss. It brought the Moravians into a close relationship with the Wesleys and, indirectly, had an effect in shaping the character of the Methodist Church. The Georgia venture also laid the basis for the formation of Moravian groups in England. And in Georgia, because of their diligence, their willingness to work, and their honesty, the Moravians earned a reputation that caused others to seek after them as colonists.

As early as 1734, when he sent Brother George Bohnisch to scout the land, Zinzendorf had considered establishing a settlement in Pennsylvania. Spangenberg had gone from Georgia to Penn's colony in 1736 for the same purpose.

By 1740 the Moravians held two tracts of land in Pennsylvania. On one of them located near the forks of the Delaware, they built the town of Nazareth. Some ten miles away on the Lehigh River they built another town which was named Bethlehem by Zinzendorf, who was visiting (as a Lutheran minister using another name) in America at the time.

The Georgia colonists and parties coming from Europe came to this area and built their towns - Bethlehem, Nazareth and Lititz were the largest - on the pattern of Herrnhut and Herrnhaag in Europe.

This transplanting of the European pattern to America undoubtedly was Zinzendorf's work. For the Count was on the ground when the plans were made. It was, in many ways, an unfortunate decision.

In Europe, where there were strong state churches, a society like the Moravians was almost compelled to live apart in separate villages. In America, however, there was no all-powerful state church (despite valiant efforts by the English to place the Anglican Church in that spot) and the logical solution was to establish congregations, not separate church villages which excluded all outsiders.

But Zinzendorf stubbornly refused to accept the fact the Moravians were a separate church. As long as he lived he considered the Brethren as nothing more than a Christian society existing within the framework of an established church. The fact there was no established church in America didn't alter Zinzendorf's views one whit.

In 1740, when the Moravians began to build their separate towns, religious forms in America had not jelled. As the Baptists, Presbyterians and Methodists were to prove, the times were ripe and the vineyards heavy laden. Had the Moravians, with their exceedingly well organized and tightly disciplined ministry, set to work organizing congregations, they probably could have become one of the great Protestant forces in America.

Instead, they turned to building their self-isolated villages on the European pattern. They transplanted the common housekeeping practices of Herrnhut to America. Instead of becoming a part of the fast moving currents in the raw, new land they remained aloof and apart and their time of opportunity passed beyond their reach.

But, by the same token, their aloofness enabled them to protect their unique ways. Most other Europeans came to America and rather quickly were transformed into something new, call that something American or frontiersman or what you will. That was not the case with the Moravians. They set out to transform the frontier by transplanting European Herrnhut into the wilderness.

The startling thing is that these curious people were surprisingly successful in that effort.

NICOLAUS LUDOVICUS COMES
A ZINZENDORF.

Nicholas Ludwig, Count Zinzendorf (1700-1760)

View of Herrnhut, 1775-1800

August Gottlieb Spangenberg (1704-1792)

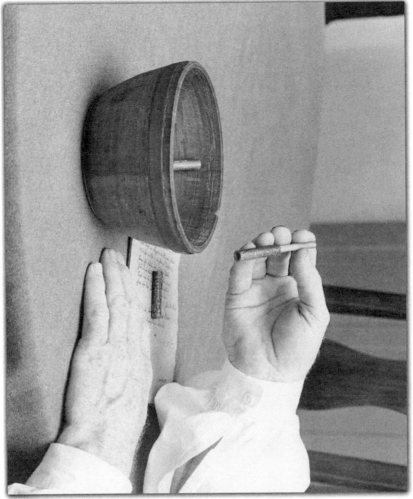

The Lot. The lot was used by the Unitas Fratrum as early as 1465 to decide questions of church policy, property, and marriage by excluding human judgment. From Biblical references, it was determined that God made the decision of the lot. The result was fair, just, and blessed. Its use cane under increasing criticism on the American frontier particularly regarding marriage and property. Democracy and the easy availability of land eventually led to separation of church and civil government in Moravian settlements in both Worlds. The marriage lot was abandoned in 1818 when its continued use became a threat to sustaining the church membership.

View of Bethlehem, Pennsylvania, 1815

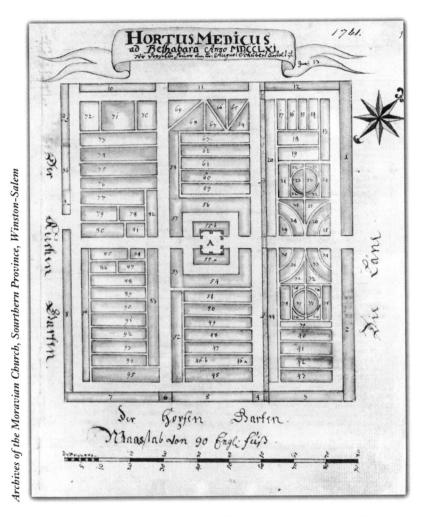

'Prospects of Bethabara,' 1759. The upland vegetable garden, center left, is enclosed by a fence. The original settler's cabin is at the extreme lower left in the garden. The floral tunnel is a grape arbor. The medical garden (Hortus medicus), the portion of the upland garden, just within the right fence border, provided the botanical drugs used for medical treatments.

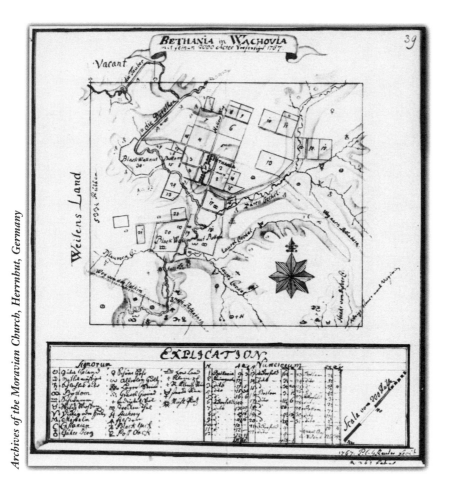

View of Bethania, 1767

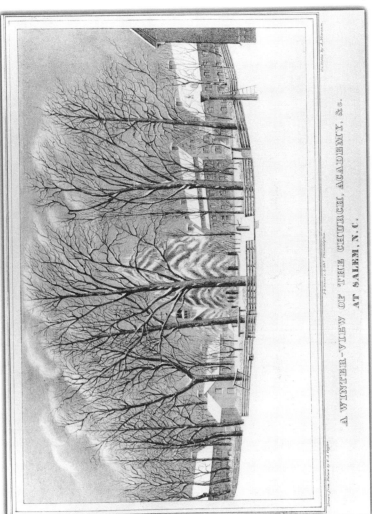

Winter view of Salem, *1850.* The Boys School is at the far left; the spire of Home Moravian Church rises in the background; Single Sisters House is at the far right, and the fire station interrupts the fence at the front of the square.

Single Brothers House on Academy Street as it stands today (2000).

C. A. Burrus

The Boys Museum on Academy Street with Home Moravian
Church in the background (2000).

A Tannenberg Organ. As it stands today in the Saal of the Single Brothers House (2000). David Tannenberg (1728-1804), a leading organ builder in early America and a truly great master of that art, emigrated from Saxony to Pennsylvania in the mid-eighteenth century. From 1765 he worked near Bethlehem in the village of Lititz, Pennsylvania making the parts of a two-manual organ for the new Home Moravian Church in Salem. The organ was assembled in North Carolina by his son-in-law, Philip Bachmann, and is now being restored. Early in 1672 Tannenberg may have been involved another organ's construction, later burned, for the congregation of the village of Bethania. The one-manual Tannenberg organ above was built in Salem in 1798 for the *Saal* (main hall) of the *Gemeine Haus* (village administrative center) and restored in 1964.

St. Philips Moravian Church, 1861. In early Salem black slaves worshiped with their owners and were buried with them in God's Acre. As a slave based economy evolved, societal pressure led to black Moravians being restricted to back seats and balconies and finally to separate churches. The first church for African-Americans was erected in 1823 and is now being reconstructed. The second, above, was erected in 1861. After emancipation, the church, called St. Philips after 1914, moved from Salem.

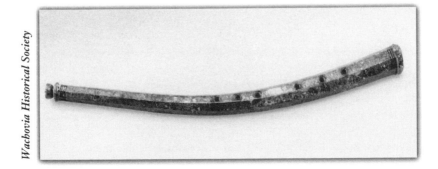

Zinke (Zincke). The zinke was a cornet-like instrument fashioned from wood, ox-horn, or ivory that was used into the eighteenth century in central Europe.

6

Spangenberg's Long Road To Wachovia

By 1750 the Moravians, because of the reputation they had gained in both Georgia and Pennsylvania, were much sought after as colonists.

Lord Granville, owner of a vast holdings in the North Carolina colony, was anxious to attract the Brethren to his grant. And, on their part, the Moravians remained interested in establishing a settlement in the southern colonies.

It was decided that August Gottlieb Spangenberg should take a party to North Carolina and search for a large tract (100,000 acres was the maximum allowed) of fertile land on a navigable river. He was to take with him men who were ". . . good and solid judges about the soil and its fertility, about the climate and its effect upon European inhabitants and their way of cultivating and manuring the land."

Brother Joseph, as Spangenberg was called, was a great man. He was born in Germany in 1704 and educated to become a Lutheran minister. In the Lutheran Church, where he protested the emphasis on cold doctrine, Spangenberg was a controversial figure. In 1733 he left Lutheranism and joined the Moravians. There he swiftly rose to become a bishop and the strong and steady right hand of Zinzendorf.

While he was a cultivated and highly educated man, Spangenberg lived a simple, rugged life. In Georgia he startled John Wesley with the ease in which he served as the congregation minister on one day and on the next worked as the village cook. He pioneered the Moravian settlements in both Georgia and Pennsylvania.

Brother Joseph chose five men to accompany him to North Carolina: Timothy Horsfield, a native of Long Island; Joseph Müller, a native of Pennsylvania who had studied medicine in Europe; Herman Loesch, the only member of the party who later lived in North Carolina; Johann Merck; and Henry Antes, the supervisor of farming, building and manufacturing at Bethlehem. All these men were relatively young and they were Moravians or, as very likely the case with Antes, men congenial to Moravian views and practices.

The party left Bethlehem on August 25, 1752, traveling to Philadelphia and then down the Eastern shore of Maryland and across into Virginia at Norfolk. "In Virginia," Spangenberg noted, "the people were fairly courteous, in Maryland less so."

The party arrived in Edenton on September 9. There Spangenberg remained for ten days, purchasing tents and other equipment and learning about the North Carolina colony from Francis Corbin, Lord Granville's obliging agent.

He quickly discovered that there was much turmoil in the colony. "...there are many cases of murder, theft and the like, but no one is punished." And, Spangenberg added, "Land matters in North Carolina also are in unbelievable confusion. A man settles on a piece of land does a good deal of work on it - from the Carolina standpoint - and then another comes and drives him out."

To make matters worse, there was no map to show just which land was claimed and which remained unclaimed. Corbin assured the Moravians, however, that there still were large tracts to be had in "the back of the colony."

Spangenberg, therefore, decided to travel west towards the Blue Mountains, today's Blue Ridge Mountains, and examine this land. By this point he knew that his original plan to locate on a navigable river was out of the question.

Shrewd and observant, Spangenberg stands in the front rank of the state's long line of interpretative reporters.

"North Carolina," he noted, "is a rather large province and the conditions of the inhabitants varies so greatly that often what is good for the Southern part is bad for the Northern part and vice versa which leads to continual strife between the sections."

He was astonished by the nature of the Carolina laws. "No Christian brought into this land can be a bond servant," he noted. "Yet, a man who helps another's slave to escape must serve the slave's owner for five years." The Bishop was particularly interested in a law which said that if a man married a person of mixed blood (Negro or Indian) he was fined fifty pounds.

But, Spangenberg added, "Here, as in all English countries, there are good laws that are not kept, but the Brethren can not act that way."

His comments on trade and commerce in North Carolina contain traces of truths which linger to this day:

-"Trade and business are poor in North Carolina. With no navigable rivers there is little shipping; with no export trade of importance the towns are few and small."

-"A good deal of tobacco is raised but it generally is taken to Suffolk or Norfolk in Virginia . . . Thus it is shipped by the Virginia merchant and the Carolinians must accept whatever prices he chooses to pay."

-"Many cattle also are sold outside of North Carolina, but the profit is in Virginia, not here. They are not killed, salted and exported from this province, but are driven to Virginia and sold on the hoof, at a loss rather than a profit."

Spangenberg noted that North Carolina hogs were driven to Virginia, sold as Virginian pork and exported in exchange for rum, sugar, molasses and the like. These things then were sold back to the North Carolinians at another profit for the Virginians. Such wastefulness caused the bishop to shake his head sadly.

Farming in North Carolina? Spangenberg noted that it was corn and hogs and that "poorly done." At one point he traveled one hundred forty miles through eastern Carolina without so much as seeing a plow or a wagon.

The settlers Spangenberg said that the native Carolinians "bear the climate well but are lazy." Of the few Scotch, Irish and English settlers he said there were two types: the first poor, honest, and hardworking and the second a lawless element attracted by the laxity of Carolina laws. Brother Joseph, perhaps because of national prejudice, was most favorably impressed by the arrival of "sturdy Germans" in the colony.

By September 18, 1752, Spangenberg, having supplied his party, drained Agent Corbin of information, and satisfied himself that any available lands must be found far to the west, prepared to start up the trading path towards the hazy shadows of the Blue Mountains.

Spangenberg and his party of five men left Edenton on September 18, 1752, starting up the trading path toward the distant Catawba towns. From what he had learned in Edenton the Bishop knew that if he was to find a large tract of fertile land still unclaimed, it would likely be somewhere in the vast forest carpet near the foot of the Blue Mountains.

The summer had been hot and dry. As the party rode west the low land about them was spotted with stagnant, scum-rimmed pools. The insects, particularly the plaguing mosquitoes, were more than annoying. They were murderous . To make matters worse the dry spell broke and torrential rains raised the rivers out of their banks, and the forests were flooded in moving water.

On September 19 Brother Merck complained of a headache. The following day Brother Antes was sick and the day after that Loesch and

Timothy Horsfield were vomiting. By the first of October, Spangenberg was stricken, first with a headache and then by chills and fever. Brother Müller, the only man in the party who escaped the fever, reported that Spangenberg ". . . burned like a heated stove."

At one point, Brother Joseph, as Spangenberg was known, was so ill that Müller almost despaired. But, he Says, "I went into the woods and talked it over with the Saviour and begged Him, if it was His will, to give Brother Joseph back to us this time."

For two weeks the party, huddled in a forest cabin, fought the fever. On October 14, with all somewhat improved except Horsfield, Spangenberg said, "We will go on in our weakness." But the weakness caused by malaria is not quickly shaken.

Five days later - days in which the Brothers alternately improved only to collapse again - the party reached Captain Senet's cabin (near what is now Hillsborough) where William Churton, the royal surveyor, and several hunters awaited them. During those five days there were times when Spangenberg had to be lifted into the saddle and, once there, held to his seat.

At Senet's the party separated. Horsfield was too ill to travel. It was decided that Müller would stay behind to nurse Horsfield while the others continued towards the Catawba River with Churton and the hunters. It was November before Horsfield was sufficiently recovered to make the long journey back to Bethlehem.

By that time Spangenberg had reached the Catawba and followed that river west to Quaker Meadows at the foot of Table Rock Mountain. In this area, Spangenberg noted, "the woods are full of Cherokees." The only trails through those woods were cut by the buffalo. Frequently the party reached streams with banks so steep that they could not be crossed "had not the buffalo broken them down here and there."

The hunters led them along the foot of the great Blue Mountains, following the Johns River for a time and then going up Big Wilson Creek to the narrow valley where the village of Edgemont now stands.

The hunters were seeking the headwaters of the "Atkin" and the hunters were lost. By late November, realizing that they were working the wrong watershed, the party left the Johns River gorge and climbed the main ridge of the mountains at a place near the present town of Blowing Bock.

It was, Spangenberg reported, "A hard journey over very high, terrible mountains and cliffs. . . . Part of the way we climbed on hands and knees." At one point a horse tumbled over backwards and fell down the mountain. A good part of the way, Spangenberg says, "We led the horses who were trembling like a leaf.

"When we reached the top we saw mountains to the right and to the left, before us and behind us, many hundreds of mountains, rising like great waves in a storm."

Early in December they stood at the headwaters of both the New and the Yadkin Rivers. Unable to distinguish the one from the other they followed the New and, within a day or so, camped near the present town of Boone. "I think," Spangenberg said, "that I never have felt a winter wind so strong and so cold."

At that point Spangenberg realized they were following the wrong stream. With little but his compass to guide him Brother Joseph turned east and south and came down out of the Blue Mountains, following tiny runs that grew into creeks and then joined larger streams that flowed into the Yadkin. On December 20 the men reached the Yadkin at a point not far above the Mulberry Fields, the site of the present Wilkesboros.

Here they found people - the first white people they had seen in weeks - and these people told them of large stretches of vacant land located to the east on the three forks of Muddy Creek.

There, on December 27, 1752, they began surveying the land they had been seeking. It was, Spangenberg said, the best land still available in North Carolina. Although there was no navigable water nearby - Spangenberg had long since given up that hope - there was enough land (just short of 100,000 acres) to meet the need. Moreover, it was reasonably fertile land. Spangenberg rated half the area as being good land and the remainder as either medium grade or poor.

Although the party examined many tracts, and even laid tentative claim to ten small pieces of land in other areas, Spangenberg felt that the Church should purchase only the Wachau tract. That name, the name of an ancestral estate of the Zinzendorfs in Austria, was selected by Spangenberg. Later, both the Moravians and their neighbors came to call the area "Wachovia."

On January 13, with the surveying completed, Spangenberg, Merck, Loesch, and Antes started back towards the northern Moravian towns, traveling the middle road (along the eastern edge of the mountains) to Pennsylvania. They arrived at Bethlehem on February 12, 1753.

Except for Henry Antes - who was stricken with an attack of gall stones shortly before the party came south, suffered a severe attack of malaria in eastern Carolina, and blood poisoning while in the mountains - these men, under-equipped as they were, came off their long and rugged winter tour of the Carolina frontier in surprisingly good shape.

It was, as Spangenberg said, a hard journey but a fruitful one.

7

Bethabara - The House of Passage

It is commonly believed that when Bishop Spangenberg recommended that the Moravian Church buy the Wachovia tract in North Carolina the church leaders, with Germanic thoroughness, went right ahead with the purchase.

Perhaps, if Spangenberg had headed the church at the time, that would have been the case. But Count Zinzendorf was the Moravian leader and by 1753 he had snarled the Moravian ball of yarn into a frightful mess. During that year the real issue was the survival of the church, not a question of whether a new settlement should be attempted in North Carolina.

The trouble began when Zinzendorf led the Moravians through what is now called the "Sifting Period." In this period, which lasted from 1743 to 1750, Zinzendorf adopted a "blood and wounds" theology which had the goal of a childlike identity with the suffering of Christ.

That theology, since it possessed a powerful appeal in the mission field, might have served a useful purpose had it been kept within reasonable limits. But, with Zinzendorf leading the way, the Moravians swiftly sailed from simple childlikeness to mawkish childishness.

As "Little Papa," Zinzendorf established "The Order of the Little Fools" and taught the Brothers and Sisters to identify themselves with the suffering of "Brother Lambkins" (Christ) on the cross.

In his biography of Zinzendorf, John R. Weinlick writes:

"Thus they spoke of themselves as 'little doves flying about in the atmosphere of the cross,' 'little fish swimming in the bed of blood,' or as 'little bees who suck on the wounds of Christ, who feel at home in the side hole and crawl in deep.' Again they would call themselves 'bloodthirsty beasts,' 'blood leeches,' 'wound worms' and 'side hole hearts.'"

The church came to be called the "visible wound church" and the Moravian hymns of this period reflected an uncommonly gruesome interest in Christ's suffering.

At the time they engaged in this aberration, the Moravians had their full share of enemies who suspected them of being separatists. Now Zinzendorf supplied those enemies with all the ammunition they possibly could use. In order to make a fool and a fanatic of the Count they needed only quote from the Count's own writings.

These excesses were one of the reasons the Moravians were evicted from Herrnhaag, the largest of their towns. Curiously, Herrnhut, oldest of the Moravian towns, was affected least. It was the new settlements, like Herrnhaag and Bethlehem in Pennsylvania, which suffered most.

During this period the Moravians made a mockery of the lot. They used it, for example, to settle such questions as whether they should build a house.

The curiosity of the "Sifting Period" was not peculiar to the Moravians. A good many of the German Pietist movements were bitten by the same bug at the same time. But among the Brethren it was particularly striking because, until that time, they had been rather successful in avoiding fanaticism.

By 1748 men like Bishop Spangenberg were thoroughly disgusted with Zinzendorf. Spangenberg resigned as the leader of the Bethlehem congregation and returned to Europe to talk with the Count. He said, "I myself was much displeased with him at the time, and he no less with me."

Under pressure brought by men like Spangenberg, the Neissers, Christian David, and other of the old leaders, Zinzendorf awoke to the fact the entire church was in danger of coming apart at the seams. He admitted his error and acted to correct the damage he had caused.

But in 1753, on the eve of the North Carolina settlement, the Moravian Church still was suffering from the after-effects of the "Sifting Period."

And by 1753 the Count had almost hopelessly snarled the financial affairs of the church.

The financial snarl came to a head in 1753 when Zinzendorf occupied Lindsey House, his headquarters in London. The Count spent 11,500 pounds sterling on Lindsey House. That investment, combined with the cost of replacing the people evicted from Herrnhaag, brought the church debt to something like 130,000 pounds, an incredible burden for such a small group.

For a time there was a likelihood that Zinzendorf and some of the other church leaders would be imprisoned for debt. That was avoided, however, and some capable businessmen took over and worked out a plan by which the church, over a period of years, could free itself of debt.

But the conditions in 1753 were such that there was little chance of the Moravians proceeding with plans of a North Carolina settlement. However, when Lord Granville learned that the venture was about to be dropped he made a second and more attractive offer. At the same time, Jonas Paulas Weiss, a German merchant, sold Zinzendorf on the plan of financing the North Carolina settlement through a land company.

A company - *Der Nord Carolina Land Und Colonie Etablissement* - was formed and shares of this company (each full share representing about two thousand acres of land in the Wachovia tract) were sold to European investors. In this manner roughly half of the 100,000-acre Wachovia tract was sold before the Moravian Brothers began their work at Bethabara.

On August 7, 1753, Earl Granville conveyed the Wachovia lands - a total of 98,985 acres - to the Moravians in nineteen separate deeds. These separate deeds protected the church. In the event they defaulted on the annual rents the Moravians did not risk seeing the entire tract revert to Lord Granville.

The terms were simple: 500 pounds sterling down and an annual rent of one hundred fifty pounds a year. Despite the Revolutionary War the Moravians paid their rent until 1788 when they purchased the quit-rents for a thousand pounds. All told, the Wachovia tract cost the church about $35,000, or about 35 cents an acre.

Later, when Lord Granville realized that there was more poor quality land in Carolina than had at first been thought, he deeded the church two additional tracts in what is now Wilkes County. Moravian Falls is located on one of those tracts. This land was sold by the church in 1778 and became involved in a law suit that dragged along until 1856.

For our purposes, however, the important fact is that the North Carolina venture was not abandoned. By late 1753 the first party of Brothers was selected to go to Wachovia and begin their building in the wilderness.

In the autumn of 1753 word came to Bethlehem from London that the Wachovia tract had been purchased from Lord Granville. The leaders of the Moravian towns in Pennsylvania went to Christiansbrunn, a farming community near Nazareth where the Single Brothers had a farm, dairy and mill, and carefully selected the party that was to make the long trip south to begin the Carolina settlement.

In the Moravian manner, two men were chosen to head the party; Bernard Adam Grube, a minister, was to watch over spiritual affairs and Jacob Loesch, also a minister, to serve as business manager. All told, fifteen men were picked to make the trip. Of these, eleven were to remain in Wachovia while four were to return to Pennsylvania where they would serve as advisers and be available to guide later parties to the "Yatkin" River country.

Each of the eleven men in the settlement party was a specialist. Hans Martin Kalberlahn, for example, was a doctor and Frederick Jacob Pfeil a shoemaker. But each in his own way also was prepared to do whatever other work was needed.

This party left Bethlehem on October 8, 1753, and headed their heavy-bodied horses and stoutwagon down a trail through Maryland and the great valley of Virginia. It was a slow, laborious journey. There were rivers, - the Potomac, James, and Dan - and innumerable small streams, often steep banked, to be crossed. Food and fodder were short. There was a bite in the November winds and on many days there was rain or a spit of snow in the air.

The Brothers entered North Carolina through what is now Stokes County and they worked their heavy wagon through the woods, around the wall of the Sauratown hills to the Wachovia tract.

On November 17, 1753, they came to a small log cabin, built by Hans Wagner and abandoned when Wagner, learning that the Moravians had purchased the land, moved on to the Yadkin River. At this place, Bethabara, meaning "The House of Passage," they stopped. That night they read the daily text (it was "I know where Thou dwellest") and held a love feast in which they shared stewed pumpkin and corn meal mush. Along with turnips and "journey cakes" this was the standard fare that first winter.

On the 18th, a Sunday, they rested; but by dawn on the 19th they went to work with a vigor which, if Colonel William Byrd's reports on "Lubberland" are to be believed, was heretofore unheard of in easy-going colonial Carolina.

Within ten days they had three acres of land cleared and were working that land with a plow built by Brother Heinrich Feldhausen.

Within five months they had planted additional land in wheat, corn, potatoes, flax, cotton, tobacco, barley, rye, oats, millet, buckwheat, turnips and pumpkins. Besides that there was a garden, neatly fenced in chestnut rails, for "salat" greens.

During the spring of 1754 the Brothers traveled among their neighbors, purchasing apple and peach trees for their orchard, swine to fatten on the oak and chestnut mast, cows (marked with an M burned on one flank and one inch cropped off the left ear) and poultry. Improvising with what they had at hand - for example, before they established a cooperage the Brothers burned barrels from tree trunks - they built a town in the middle of a howling nowhere. Except for a very few items - salt, coffee, glass and nails - it was a self-supporting town.

In these very early days the Brothers were bothered less by Indians, insects and wild beasts than they were by nosy neighbors. Brother Grube confessed, "It is very inconvenient for us to entertain strangers for our space is small and we have nothing for them to sleep on." Yet as he admitted, "Nearly every day we have some extra people to feed."

These people came to Bethabara to gawk at the eleven Brothers and they came also to visit the doctor. The early diary is filled with notations such as "An Irishman came to have a tooth pulled." The visitors came also to ask the tailor to make them a pair of leather breeches or to buy a pair of brogans from the shoemaker. Later they came to purchase nails from the smith, earthenware from the potter, and wine and brandy from the distiller. Brother Hans Petersen, as *Fremden Diener*, served as official host to the visitors.

This trade, drawn from many miles around, grew as a store was opened and other craftsmen - a gunsmith, for example - came down from Pennsylvania. In the very beginning most of the trade was in kind. When neighbor Abraham Wilson cut his foot, for example, Dr. Kalberlahn patched him up for a fee of two cows. Another time two German visitors agreed to fell one hundred trees and make three thousand shingles for two pair of shoes. "We not only had enough for ourselves," the Moravians said, "but were able to help many hundreds of people who came to us from sixty miles away.

Because this parade of visitors inconvenienced them, often causing a Brother to sit out the "night watch" while some stranger snored in his bed, the first new building at Bethabara was a small log cabin guest house.

As a matter of fact, the first school at Bethabara was established for the benefit of neighbors. In those early years the Brothers and Sisters who came to Wachovia left their children behind. The only children of school age in the area were those of the neighbors.

The important thing, whether they worked for themselves or for their neighbors, was the unending diligence that marked these quiet people.

It is commonly said that in a communal society - a society in which each man contributes according to his ability and shares according to his need - there is no incentive for a fellow to hump along any harder than is absolutely essential. But that is not necessarily the case; and you need only look to the bee, the ant, and the Moravian for proof of the fact.

Consider, for example, the case of John Jacob Friis, who came from Bethlehem to serve as pastor at Bethabara in 1754. His diary reflects the spirit of those first days. For, along with his pastoral duties, Brother Friis served as a jack of many trades.

On April 29, 1754, he reports, "I sought swine the whole afternoon...For the first time put on Indian shoes, they are light but my feet are yet too tender."

On a day when he had been carving table feet in the shape of a lion's claws, Friis philosophized, "One day I am a joinor and the next a carver; what could I not learn if I was not too old?" On yet another day he recorded, "I am your first cowherd in North Carolina."

These jottings from the pastor's diary capture the spirit of the time:

July 3- Friis helps bring in flax.

July 4- Friis serves as village cook.

July 6- Friis picks blackberries to make vinegar.

July 12- "I was the watcher of the fowl. At this work one must be very brisk and active."

July 13- "I cleaned the yard and sleep hall."

July 16- "We have smoked for a fortnight our new tobacco. It grows incomparably well."

Among the other Brothers it was the same. As a result, by the close of 1755, Bethabara was solidly established. There was a *Gemeinhaus* (Meeting House), a two-story Single Brothers' House, a mill, a smithy, a cooperage, two bridges, a tool house, a brick kiln, a pottery, tannery, wash house, tailor's shop and six houses in the village plus a house at the mill for the miller and his guests. Considerable acreage of land had been cleared and planted. Roads had been cut to the Yadkin and to connect with the main road to Salisbury. More than that the Brethren had surrounded Bethabara with a palisade.

As colonists on the lonely frontier these beaverish fellows were unequalled.

8

White Men in the Land of Red Gods

We customarily think of the Moravians as a townspeople; and that they were. But in Wachovia they built their towns from a forest and we sometimes overlook their dependence on that forest.

When they came into the Yadkin Valley in the late fall of 1753 they found that the hickory was the most common tree. It provided them with their finest firewood. From the nuts they got an oil-rich food and they crushed the hickory hulls with alum and made a strong yellow dye.

The stick-straight yellow poplar, with its soft but even-grained wood, provided fine boards for their buildings. "Often four or five logs for planks," they reported.

Black walnut, a tree of the bottom lands, was the richest grained of the Wachovia woods. In the early days it was not an uncommon tree. Bethania, the farming community established in 1759, was built in what the Moravians called the Black Walnut Bottoms.

The chestnut, another common tree, was valuable for its mast, which men ate and also used to fatten hogs and even diced and dried and made do as a substitute for coffee. This easily split and weather-resistant wood was favored for fence rails and for the shakes they used to shingle their roofs.

The baker preferred ash wood for his oven and the wagon maker prized ash because it was strong and turned well on a lathe. It was commonly thought that ash kept snakes away.

In the late winter, when the sap began to rise, the Brothers tapped the maples and boiled sugar. This custom, however, did not last. After 1764 it was cheaper to buy sugar imported from the West Indies. For this sugar, as for the other things they could not produce, they traded deer skins and the products of their craftsmen.

There were a wide variety of oaks in Wachovia and each had its special uses. White oak was best for mast, since its acorns were sweet. It was favored by the potter for his kiln. Post oak was a good wagon wood. Black oak was used, along with white oak, in building. The sap of Spanish oak, tapped in the spring, was used to make vinegar. And willow oak was sought by the tanner for its acid bark.

Red beech, a tree of the valleys, was preferred by the distiller for his fires; and the cooper sought the water beech, which drew well beneath his cutting knife.

They made baskets from the creek-side willows and they used the shredded bark of the pap-paw for cord. The bark of the alder and the wood of the sumac bush were sources of dye. From the berries of the forest they made wine and, until they established their own orchards, they relied on the persimmon, the wild plum, the black haw and the wild cherry for fruit. They were astonished that in the Blue Mountains, as Spangenberg said, "Many hundreds of thousands of wild apple trees, crab apples . . . . grew wild."

The pines, of course, were important to them in making fine, flat boards. They looked also to the sourwood trees and their visitors, the wild bees.

In time they established an apothecary's shop in Bethabara. But in the first days the floor of the forest around them provided them with their drugs.

The snakeroots were used to purify the blood and as an antidote for venom. Tea made from the leaves of the holly tree was given for fevers. Milkweed was used to treat pleurisy and squawsweed was a specific for rheumatism.

For fresh wounds they used the carpenter leaf and for open wounds they bound on the leaves of the night shade. Water cress (also calves foot root) was rated good for lung trouble and a tea made of maidenhair fern was used to treat coughs.

The pith of the bullrush provided them with a wick for their oil lamps and they purged their horses with a dose made from the may apple.

Later, when Dr. Kalberlahn had planted an herb garden, the Moravians came to rely less on the forest. But in the early years that reliance was more a part of the Moravian story than most of us have appreciated.

Curiously, the Moravians were disappointed by the lack of fine building stone in Wachovia. "Even in the mountains," Spangenberg said, "there is not one-tenth as much stone as we find everywhere in Pennsylvania."

Sometimes, perhaps for the sporting climb, they went to Pilot Mountain in search of whet stones. Brothers Ettwein and Gammern climbed the pinnacle of Pilot Mountain in April, 1763. Most often however, the Brethren got their sharpening stones from "whet stone hill," which was located no more than three miles from Bethabara.

Although they knew of traces of silver and lead in Wachovia, the Moravians did not mine. Except for clay and the quarrying of building stone they did not dig into their land.

But they found excellent clays near all their towns and they soon made building brick, earthenware, tile for their roofs (fearing fire, the Moravians distrusted wooden shingles) and fine tile for their most ingenious and effective tile stoves. On the day the kilns were opened neighbors flocked to Wachovia to buy jugs, plates, platters and **the** like by the wagon load.

They were handicapped, of course, by many lacks. From the first they imported salt, sugar, coffee, glass and, until their smithy, was built nails. One of the most nagging lacks was the absence of lime in Wachovia. Because of that shortage they were compelled to build with naked boards where they would have preferred to have used plaster. Oftentimes their wagons, returning from the coastal towns, were loaded with sea shells which they burned to obtain lime.

In their organized manner, a manner colored by their European background, the Moravians prized the forest and the wealth it provided them. Even in the early days one Brother was appointed a forester and he controlled the cutting of the trees on a selective basis.

Two centuries ago on the American frontier such conservation was unheard of. To the first settlers the forest was an enemy to be pushed back and destroyed. But, to the Moravians the forest was a friend; and they used the forest well and profited in that use.

When sportsmen gather to complain of the evil times that have come upon them, there is much wistful talk of "the good old days" when the streams, filled with fish, ran green and clear through forest that shaded great herds of game.

The Moravians, who were among the first to settle in the Piedmont, saw this land as it was in the beginning and they recorded what they saw. From those reports it is plain that early Wachovia was not the sportsman's paradise we sometimes think.

To begin with, there were game laws even then. While these laws, like so many North Carolina laws of that time, probably were not enforced, they, at least, raise some questions regarding any great abundance of game.

In 1752 there was a five pound sterling fine for killing deer between February 15 and July 15. Moreover, only landowners - and, then, only landowners who cultivated at least five thousand hills of corn - were permitted to hunt for deer.

Some game, however, was so abundant as to be pestiferous. In 1768, for example, the General Assembly required all land owners to kill at least seven squirrels or crows each year, or else, pay a penalty.

When Spangenberg made his exploratory tour of western North Carolina in 1752 he reported abundant buffalo sign in the vicinity of Table Rock Mountain. The elk were gone but deer were common throughout the area. "There are," Spangenberg said, "many hunters here who work little, live like the Indians, shoot many deer, and sell their skins."

Black bear were numerous in Wachovia and so were wolves -black and gray - and wild turkey. "The wolves and bear," Spangenberg noted, "must be exterminated if cattle raising is to succeed." As late as 1774, a year of a killing spring freeze, one of the Brothers noted that "panthers have been seen several times." That year both the Moravians and the Royal Governor offered a bounty of ten shillings for killing a panther.

The Moravians, who never were much as hunters or fishermen killed their first game in Wachovia (two wild turkeys) on November 18, 1753. (Besides being the day after the settlement party arrived in Wachovia, it also was a Sunday.) On the 20th, Brother Feldhausen walked into the woods and got lost. He returned on the 21st proudly shouldering the carcass of a deer.

Because they were not accomplished hunters the Moravians soon came to rely more on professional hunters - the "long hunters" of the frontier - than on their own skills.

The diaries are filled with the mention of a shortage of game. In 1752 Spangenberg commented, "There is little game to be found." In 1754 John Jacob Friis noted, "There is not much game here." In December, 1756, another Brother reported, "A bear hunter brought his gun to our gunsmith. He complained that neither he nor his companions had seen a single bear - all the hunters say the same."

There were years, however, when the mast crop failed. Then the animals - bears, wolves and panthers - visited the Moravian towns seeking food. Each loss, whether it be a lamb, a sheep, a calf or a hog, was duly reported in the diary. In those first years such losses were common.

The Moravians did some trapping and some skin hunting. They dug pits for wolves late in 1754 and caught two wolves in February, 1775. They also trapped a few beaver in Wachovia and took some raccoon, muskrat (which they sold as young beaver), opossum, bobcat, and mink.

Skunk were common enough. Of this animal they said, "He who comes near is horribly repaid by what is thrown out."

In the main, however, they left hunting and trapping to the professionals with whom they traded. Deer skins were the big item. On March 15, 1765, the Moravians sent five wagons loaded with 9,400 pounds of deer skins from Bethabara to Charlestown. That same year two hunters, who came to Bethabara from across the mountains, left 1,600 pounds of deer skins at the store.

Passenger pigeons were "numerous" in Wachovia, "especially in the Winter." "In the Fall [of 1760] there were most unusual numbers of wild pigeons here. In many places the woods where they rested for the night were ruined and the droppings were, here and there, shoe top deep."

Men went to the roosting places and killed 1,200 to 1,800 pigeons on a single hunt. "Pigeons go off in clouds," they said, and "trees that have withstood many a heavy storm fall to the ground beneath their weight."

Partridge or quail, "small but delicate of flavor," were common. Turkey and duck, particularly wood duck, were "often numerous." Pheasant - the ruffed grouse - was described as "rare," but wild geese "come every year" and flocks of turtle dove were common.

Some of the more exotic birds and animals fascinated the Moravians. They noted that the whippoorwill "calls only at night" and they commented on a curious squirrel which had "short wings like a bat."

Although the streams were filled with fish, a fact Spangenberg duly recorded, the Brothers spent little time angling for them. They caught their first fish in March, 1756, in the mill race at Bethabara. Later, whenever the mill pond was drained, they were on hand to capture the fish left floundering in the shallows.

In the Yadkin, which they said "swarms with fish," there were pike, perch, eels, white fish, rock fish, or "cableau," and what they called "shott fish." They said there were sturgeon in the Roanoke and they noted that the carp, a fish which they knew in Europe, was not found in Wachovia.

Along with the varmints and the food animals and fish there were also the deadly ones.

In May, 1762, rabies broke out in Wachovia. "As a matter of precaution most of the Brothers and Sisters were bled."

Worst of all were the snakes; the rattlesnake, copper snake and a snake they called the "pastoral" which, they said, "looks like a rattlesnake and its bite is just as bad but it has not rattle."

In 1770 one Brother wrote, "In our neighborhood many have been killed by snakes; in Bethania a medium sized rattlesnake coiled itself about a child's leg and one of the Sisters tore it away with her bare hands without receiving any injury and before it hurt the child."

So it was in those early wilderness days. Wild beasts meant danger and loss, perhaps, even death, but they also provided food and not a little pleasure to the Moravians. As they cleared the forest the life within the forest changed. Many species - the elk (gone before they came), buffalo, panther, wolf, beaver, and bear - vanished from Wachovia. But there were others, the ones which lived comfortably with man like the quail, rabbit and mourning dove, which became more abundant.

The sun of the Red Gods was setting when the Moravians first came to North Carolina.

In the eastern sections of the state the tribes were scattered. "The Chowan Indians," Bishop Spangenberg noted, "are reduced to a few families and their land has been taken from them." It was much the same with the once proud and powerful Tuscarora. Bewildered by the white man and his ways, Spangenberg said, "the Indians. . . . are as uncertain as fowls of the air."

In the west, however, it was different. Along the great inland rivers the Catawbas still held to their towns. Beyond them, in the land of the Blue Ridge, Spangenberg reported "the woods are full of Cherokees" and there always was the danger of encountering a wandering party of northern Indians, perhaps Shawnees or Senecas, loping along in search of trouble.

To the Moravians these western Indians were "wild men"; and there were times, when the tribes painted for war, the gentle Brethren of Wachovia knelt in prayer with loaded muskets at their side.

Mission work among the Indians was one of the reasons the Moravians came to America and settled in Georgia, Pennsylvania and North Carolina. Many of the Moravian leaders, men like Bishop David Nitschmann, David Zeisberger (who spent 60 years among the Six Nations), Christian Henry Rauch, (who translated several books into the Delaware tongue) and even Zinzendorf, worked in this sometimes bloody field.

For the Moravians the worst of the troubles came during the French and Indian Wars. From 1754 until 1770, when the Cherokees "sold" their lands in the Treaty of Sycamore Shoals, there was trouble.

In the beginning it was worse in the North. On November 24, 1755, the Moravian mission town of Gnadenhutten in Pennsylvania was attacked. Ten persons were killed; seven missionaries, two missionary wives and a baby belonging to one of the couples. The wife of one of the missionaries was carried off by the Indians. Only a few escaped.

The Indian attacks in the northern colonies caused many families to pull their stakes and move to Carolina. As the new settlers encroached upon the Indian lands the Cherokee, traditionally friends of the English, grew restive and, at length, warlike.

Bethabara and, after 1759, the new farming village of Bethania became places of refuge for settlers terrified by Indian raids and rumors of raids.

In 1755 a palisade was built around Bethabara. Manakes Hill, which overlooked the village, was cleared of trees and the forest was pushed back from around the village itself The Bethabara mill was fortified and ten houses were built there to house refugees.

Despite their age-old scruples against bearing arms, the Moravians established a "watch" – which the governor misinterpreted as a "militia"- headed by Brother Jacob Loesch. When there were Indians in the area, the Brothers, with guns in hand, sounded blasts on their trumpets and rang the village bell to warn the "wild men" that they were alert.

Although Bethabara and Bethania never were attacked, there were constant alarms.

In May, 1755, for example, two bands of Cherokee visited the mill at Bethabara. There was no trouble but these same bands had robbed and stolen elsewhere along the frontier. As was their custom - the Indians knew the Moravians as an easy "touch" - the Brothers fed the visitors and sent them on their way with prayers that they would go and sin no more.

A year later Jacob Loesch was stopped in the woods by a band of eleven Indians. These warriors, probably a party that had come down from the North, held a white woman as a prisoner and they attempted to capture Brother Loesch's horse. He held them off with a pointed gun. Contrary to the traditions of western fiction there is no record that the Brothers later attempted to free the captured white woman.

In 1757 Indians raided within thirty miles of Wachovia. Although conditions eased somewhat in 1758, Shawnees raided along the North Carolina frontier and the problem of housing refugees was acute in Wachovia.

In April of 1759, four persons were killed by northern Indians on the Yadkin not thirty miles from Wachovia. In May, one Brother reported, "There is a great fear all through the land." That year Bethabara frequently housed as many refugees as there were villagers.

By the spring of 1760 the Cherokees were on the warpath. William Fish and his son, who lived in "The Hollow," the place we now call Mount Airy, were killed. Another man, who had been with Fish, came to Bethabara to be treated for an arrow wound. That spring more than fifteen neighbors of the Moravians were killed. In March, for example, fast moving bands of Indians raided to within eight miles of the Moravian towns.

On March 14, 1760, the watchman at Bethania spotted an Indian spying on the village and shot at him. A party of refugees traveling the three miles between Bethabara and Bethania narrowly escaped capture; and two neighbors who left the mill at Bethabara and returned to their farms were killed and scalped.

During 1760 Brothers who traveled between Bethania and Bethabara rode at a dead gallop and caused the red men to curse the Dutchmen and their fort and their great horses.

After 1761 there no longer was trouble in Wachovia or along the Yadkin. There were, however, sporadic outbursts of raiding in the mountains, particularly in the New River country, as more and more white settlers pushed into lands reserved for the tribes.

While the Indian attacks amounted to little more than hit and run raids against isolated cabins - the war parties refused to tackle a strong place like Bethabara and their attack on Fort Dobbs (near Statesville) in 1760 was unsuccessful - the white men were most efficient. Troops marched against the Cherokee towns and those towns were leveled down to the last hill of corn. The war power of the Cherokee, last of the great tribes, was broken.

They were, Bishop Spangenberg said, "scattered as the wind scatters smoke."

9

The Brethren's Road to Salem

It is possible, had it not been for the Indian troubles, that the Moravians might have developed a way of life in Wachovia quite different from that in Herrnhut or in the Pennsylvania towns. The original plan was to establish families on adjoining farms rather than in a village. Moreover, it was at first intended that the *oeconomie* - the common household economy - would be relaxed just as quickly as these farms could be settled and the families were able to care for their own needs.

But the Indian troubles compelled the Moravians to live close to one another in a village for mutual protection; and those same Indian troubles caused the Brethren to continue their communal economy far longer than they had at first intended.

By 1759, despite the French and Indian War, Church leaders authorized the building of a second town nearby. Bishop Spangenberg, visited Wachovia to select the site in Black Walnut Bottom about three miles from Bethabara. Here, in the summer of 1759, eight Moravian couples and eight couples of "the Society" (not members of the Moravian Church, but persons who wished to share the Moravian way of life) built the farming village of Bethania.

By 1759 the Moravians enjoyed certain special privileges. Ten years before, the British Parliament specifically recognized the Moravians as an "ancient, Protestant Episcopal Church." The Moravians were one of the few churches to receive such special treatment.

When Wachovia was established some of the Brothers believed this new land should be made into a special county. Spangenberg, however, opposed this, pointing to the Moravian scruples against the taking of an oath or bearing arms. How could we, he asked, seek to be made into a special county when we will not serve on juries or in the militia?

As a compromise, the Colonial Assembly placed Wachovia in a special parish - it was named after Governor Arthur Dobbs - and excused the

Brethren from taking oaths and from bearing arms. The Brethren tended to their affairs in Dobbs Parish but they left the affairs of the colony and of their own county to other hands.

With this arrangement the Moravians were able to continue their peculiarly dedicated lives within the framework of the Anglican Church. In the new land of North Carolina they continued to observe their ancient customs.

Their first Children's Christmas Service (held for the children of neighbors, many of whom had never attended a Christmas Service) was celebrated inside the stockade at Bethabara. In 1762 they held their first Candlelight Love Feast. On March 26, 1758, they held their first Easter Sunrise Service on the *Hutberg* (Manakes Hill) beside the tiny grave of Anna Maria Opiz. On that morning "The congregation was awakened early with music," and "as they sang the sun broke through a bank of clouds, throwing its clear beams upon the scene."

There were the reading meetings in which the congregation gathered at the *Gemeinhaus* to hear the news from Herrnhut, the foreign missions and from the Pennsylvania towns.

Each day the daily text was read at the evening *Singstunde*. During the worst of the Indian troubles the Hourly Intercession was revived and selected Brothers and Sisters, hour by hour, prayed throughout the day and night.

As the villages grew and the choirs were established the numbers of love feasts increased. At one time the entire congregation would assemble for a love feast. At another time it would be the Single Sisters or the Single Brothers and, at still another, the Single Sisters who were spinners would have a love feast of their own.

While the Moravians did not dress in a manner that was peculiar, there were certain touches in their customs which set them apart from their neighbors.

A little girl, for example, wore a net cap tied under the chin by a pink ribbon. When that girl grew older and became a member of the church she changed to a white cap tied with a red ribbon.

Single Sisters wore white linen caps tied with pink ribbons, Married Sisters used a blue ribbon while the Widow's ribbon was white. The Brothers dressed in the manner of their neighbors, with shoes, breeches, a shirt and hat sufficing in warm weather.

When Bethabara and Bethania were young, the days, each one recorded in the diaries, were filled with the record of small triumphs and family sorrows.

In February, 1754, the diarist reported that a brother had fashioned a trumpet from the limb of a tree. "No trumpet in Bethlehem," he boasted, "has a better tone."

Only a month before, the diary reported that the small cabin at Bethabara had caught on fire; that Brother Petersen had been hurt while felling a tree for "the visitors'" house, and that Dr. Kalberlahn had scalded his foot.

Occasionally the rise and fall of this pattern of events and accidents was broken by tragedy. Then the men took their horns from their cases and sped a departing spirit on its way.

Disease was the most serious problem in Wachovia. Each fall there was an outbreak of fever. The "bloody flux" was common and sometimes fatal. The first three Moravian children born in Wachovia died in their first year.

The greatest tragedy occurred in 1759 when refugees brought typhus fever to Bethabara. The first to die was Mary Rogers, wife of an English minister in Wachovia. In Bethabara alone eight died, fourteen others came close to "going home," and still another twenty were exceedingly sick. That year only nineteen persons escaped this epidemic, which took the lives of Dr. Kalberlahn and his patient, the Rev. Christian Seidel, within two days of one another.

But, despite such serious setbacks, the community continued to expand. Trade was established with the eastern towns, first with Charlestown and later with Cross Creek, the place we now call Fayetteville. And the craftsmen of Bethabara - the tanner, potter, joiner, cooper, gunsmith, distiller, storekeeper, and the others - attracted visitors from throughout the area.

This very prosperity, however, was a source of trouble.

On the one hand it aroused jealousy among some of the neighbors. There were those who had said that the Moravians spread smallpox by inoculation. Customs such as the Easter Sunrise Service were regarded with suspicion by the neighbors of these seemingly strange people.

There was, on the other hand, a growing restlessness among the Brethren. In some instances a Brother failed to keep his human nature fully in step with the day-to-day pattern of Christian living. In 1762, for example, Brother Feldhausen, the distiller, ". . . yielded to carnal desires and fell into all kinds of sin and shame." Some of the young men and young women became engaged to persons outside the congregation and failed to seek the permission of the village elders.

Then there were others who rebelled at being made to go to the common store and ask for what they and the members of their family needed. For in those days if a man wished to build a cabinet he was required to go to the store, state his purpose and request that he be given the necessary planks and tools.

As time passed, some Brethrens saw their neighbors enjoying growing "American individualism" and chaffed at church regulations that guided all community life. But in the first decade of Wachovia, of the 125 Moravians who arrived to settle, only eight were dismissed or chose to live elsewhere.

In fact, Bethabara was going so well that church authorities in Europe had to specifically direct that the time had come to begin work on the central town, the place Count Zinzendorf said should be named Salem. And they sent brother Frederick William Marshall to see that their instructions would be carried out.

Late in 1764 parties led by Brother Marshall, *oeconomus* or chief executive of the North Carolina settlement, explored the central area of the Wachovia tract seeking a site for the town they were to call Salem.

Several sites were found but when the question was put to the lot the answer was "No." On February 14, 1765, however, the lot was favorable. So also was the place selected. It was on a hill and yet shielded from the north winds and sufficiently high to be free from the floods and the malaria that plagued life at Bethabara.

In May of that year Christian Gottlieb Reuter surveyed the site and plans were made to finance the new town. It was agreed that the Salem congregation should be given 3,159 acres of land and that for five years this land should be rent free. Money for the town building was raised by the sale of land elsewhere in the Wachovia tract.

By January, 1766, a road, over which brick and planks could be hauled, had been built across the six miles that separated Bethabara from the Salem site. On January 6 men began to fell trees on the site. The daily text of that day was from the book of Isaiah and promised, "I will defend this city."

On January 19 a party of eight Single Brothers - two Danes, two Germans and four born in the Pennsylvania settlements - moved to the site (along the way they shot two deer) and, as an earlier town building party had done at Bethabara in 1753, settled in a log cabin.

At the outset there were plans for ten buildings in Salem: a *Gemeinhaus* to serve both as a meeting place and as a residence for the minister, a Single Brothers house, a Single Sisters house, a store, tavern, pottery, a home for the smith, and the gunsmith, an apothecary, a mill and sawmill and a farm with a barn large enough for "about 10 cows. This was to be the nucleus of the new town.

Work on the first house, a one-story structure with a loft located on Main Street, began in June, 1766. Within five years the Moravians, working with their customary energy, had laid out and built the largest part of the town they planned. The planning and most of the construction was directed by Frederick William Marshall, one of the first of North Carolina's master builders.

At the close of 1766 there were one hundred thirty persons living in Bethabara and another eighty-seven in Bethania. Except for the building crew Salem had no residents.

Six years later Salem had a population of one hundred twenty, Bethabara had shrunk to fifty-four and there were one hundred five persons living in Bethania.

The shift from Bethabara to Salem was gradual but it reached its peak late in 1771 and early 1772. The *Gemeinhaus* in Salem was consecrated on November 13, 1771. On that day the Salem congregation began its separate existence. The Salem diary begins at this time. Because of the influence of Marshall, who favored the use of the English language, the diary was written in English for ten years. Then the brothers reverted to German and did not write again in English until 1857.

In 1772 the church administration was moved from Bethabara to Salem. Brother Bagge and his wife moved to take over the Salem Store. Brother and Sister Meyer moved from Bethabara to open the Salem tavern. Surveyor Reuter and his wife also moved to the new town. In April of that year Sister Elizabeth Oesterlein held the first day school for girls in Salem. In the spring of 1772 the diarist at Bethabara reported. "Within the last days good Bethabara has given 19 of its dear residents to Salem."

That was according to the plan. Salem, the central town, was to be the commercial and manufacturing hub of Wachovia. Bethabara and Bethania and, later, Friedland and Friedberg were to remain essentially farming communities.

By 1773-the year work was begun boring out white oak logs and laying Salem's unique water System - the new town was truly the center of the Wachovia settlement. The professional men - the doctor, apothecary, and surveyor - lived there. Salem also was the craft and manufacturing center where the mason, carpenter, sawyer, cabinet maker, wagon maker, weaver, potter, distiller, tanner, smiths (black, gun, lock, nail and silver), midwife and nurse, bookkeeper, night watchman, and others plied their trades.

These crafts continued to expand. Brother Miksch, for example, opened a tobacco shop in the early days of Salem and, thereby, began a tradition that was to become important in the new town. Signs were hung from the shops - "Gottfried Aust-Potter," for example - to advise strangers of the wares and services available to them. Besides being the craft center, the Brothers House boasted a brewery, a bakery and a butcher's shop.

Because they lived apart from others, the residents of Salem-like those of Bethabara and Bethania-continued to be the target of rumors. In 1773,

and just at harvest time, too, it was whispered that there was smallpox in
Salem. These rumors, the Brethren confessed, described their way of life in
the "most unpleasant colors. "These rumors became even more unpleasant
as relations between the Colonists and the Royal Governor became
increasingly strained.

While most of the village visitors were well behaved, there always were
exceptions. Sharpshooters visited the Wachovia towns and used the tavern
as a place for passing their counterfeit money. In a time when the currency
included Johannes, doubloons, Spanish pistoles, moidres, English guineas,
ducats, pounds sterling, and pistoreens, to name but a few, the tavern
keeper, besides being a diplomat, needed more than a casual knowledge of
minting and the ways of rascals.

Fights were not uncommon in the tavern, where strangers sometimes
gathered and drank more stout Moravian brandy than was good for them.
On one occasion in August, 1772, two men fell to fighting in the streets and
when a third man intervened the pair turned on the Samaritan and broke
his leg. In those days the residents of Salem spoke often of the lawless
visitors who robbed travelers and stole livestock, calling them "the evil
men."

When Salem was established there was, except for the Moravians, little
in the way of religion in the Yadkin Valley country. In 1766 one brother
commented, "At this time the Baptists are the only ones in the country who
go far and wide preaching and caring for souls."

Whether people liked it or not - and they sometimes didn't -the
Moravians roamed among their neighbors preaching. Brother Utley
traveled among the settlers and preached both in English and German. For
several years George Soelle was a most diligent itinerant minister. Brother
Soelle, by the way, was himself an interesting commentary on the
Moravians' peculiar lack of enthusiasm for bringing persons of different
faiths into their congregation.

Soelle was a Lutheran. He joined the Moravians because their simple
way of life appealed to him. But when it came to joining the Moravian
Church, Soelle was discouraged. "They recommended," he said, "that I
remain where I was and there serve the Saviour."

10

Sing a Song of Six Pence...

The Moravians, who patterned their way of life on the ways of the primitive Christians, were communists. They practiced communism four hundred years before Karl Marx came along to lay the basis for the present-day Russian experiment. That experiment and the Moravian version of communism have, however, little in common except the name.

Until Salem was founded the Moravians maintained a strict form of common housekeeping which they called the *oeconomie*. The means of production - the land and tools and machinery - were owned by the community and the goods they produced were shared by the community. In Wachovia men contributed to the common goods according to their ability and they shared from the community's stock of common goods according to their need.

If there were shortages the elders of the church ordered rationing. In the early days at Bethabara, for example, butter was scarce. The elders determined the precise amount of butter each person should be allowed; a woman with child was permitted more butter each week than a Single Sister and a man working in the fields was given more than a Brother doing lighter work.

There were two stores in Bethabara, one for strangers and one for members of the congregation. The Brethren went to the congregation store and asked only for what they needed. At the public store strangers purchased whatever they wished and could pay for.

Even professional men like Dr. Kalberlahn in Bethabara worked for the community.

This rigid economy, which was continued for longer than the Moravians intended because of the Indian unrest, was a source of trouble. In May, 1765, for example, Dr. August Schubert left Bethabara because he (1) objected to working on the community farm and (2) resented being required to go to the store and ask for those things his family needed. Complaints of this sort were rather common.

After 1759, when Bethania was founded, there was some relaxation in the strict controls. As Brother Marshall observed, "Although Bethabara and Bethania lie close together there is a great difference in their methods as if they were far apart. Bethania does things as they come. Bethabara plans."

But the real change did not occur until after 1772 when the Salem economy had reached full stride. But even in Salem the controls remained exceedingly rigid by present day standards.

The basis of the Moravian economic system in Wachovia was the land. In each village the land belonged to the congregation. In Salem, for example, lots were not sold. Instead, the lots were leased with the understanding the lease would be renewed so long as the tenant remained acceptable to the congregation.

In this manner the church determined just who lived in the village. No one was admitted to Salem unless it was felt he had something to contribute to the community and he, in his turn, agreed to abide by the town's customs.

While a person living in Salem did not own his land he did have title to any improvements which he put on that land (the improvements, of course, first being approved by the elders). When he left Salem - or was dismissed from the congregation - he was permitted to sell the improvements at a stipulated price to some person the congregation approved or, there being no buyer, to the congregation itself. An unauthorized sale meant a stiff one hundred pounds sterling fine.

Affairs in Salem were controlled by two groups.

The *Aeltesten Conferenz* was responsible for the spiritual affairs of the congregation. Only this group could use the lot.

In 1772 the *Aufseher Collegium* was established to look after the secular - largely financial - affairs of the community. The functions of the *Collegium* were much like those of a present-day Board of Aldermen.

There was, at least for a time, a third group known as the *Grosse Helfer Conferenz*, which was composed of members of the other two bodies. It had no specific powers but, rather, served as the eyes of the community much in the manner of a grand jury. What it observed it reported to the appropriate authorities for attention.

These groups exerted astonishing controls.

The *Aeltesten Conferenz*, for example, watched over all religious affairs along with such matters as marriage, relations with neighbors, community behavior and the like. The following notes taken from the diary of the Salem *Conferenz* are rather typical.

April 6, 1774- "It shall be recommended to Peter Rose that he marry Rosina Bockel."

April 7, 1774- "Peter Rose has not accepted the proposal concerning Rosina Bockel but suggests Sister Christine Merk. The *Aeltesten Conferenz* considers it necessary to send on the proposal to her through Sister Graff." "On the 8th Sister Merk positively declined, as she is not fitted for work on a plantation." "Brother Peter Rose thereupon accepted the first suggestion, and Sister Rosina Bockel accepted it."

The *Aufseher Collegium* was just as authoritative. It set wages and the price to be paid for items in the store and in the craft shops. It selected the wood to be cut in the forest and put a price on that wood. When Brother Aust, the potter, dug clay from land belonging to the Single Sisters' choir he was told the price he must pay and what he must do to repair the land when his digging was done.

The *Collegium* set the postal rates, watched over weights and measures, and supervised the town's water system, police and fire protection, sanitation and the like.

When a new craftman was needed in the village - in 1773, for example, Salem needed a tanner - the *Collegium* made the arrangements. When the apothecary, a poor manager, had financial trouble the *Collegium* advised him. When, as sometimes happened, square pegs got in round holes, the *Collegium* made the necessary adjustments.

In Salem, however, the old communal ways were relaxed into a form of socialism.

Brothers and Sisters were permitted to set up separate housekeeping. When Governor William Tryon and his wife visited Wachovia in 1767 they were delighted to learn that individual Moravians could hold private property. The Governor was particularly happy to discover that the Moravians were plowing their earnings back into the development of Wachovia rather than exporting them to Europe as was commonly rumored.

The craftsmen, professional men and others now worked for themselves. Except for the rental they paid on the land they leased (and that rental took the place of taxes in Salem), their earnings belonged to them rather than to the community. Within a relatively short time some brothers - John Vogler was one - were quite well-to-do.

However, certain businesses - the store, the tavern, the tannery, the two farms, the pottery and the mill - continued to be operated for the benefit of the community. At the mill, for example, the miller received one third of the toll outright. The remaining two thirds was divided, with one fourth going to the miller and the rest to the community.

Curiously, within this community economy were also found the separate economies of the Brothers and Sisters Houses. These choir economies (they were called diaconies) were headed by a business manager or *vorsteher* who worked through the *Aufseher Collegium.*

In a sense, these choir diaconies provided North Carolina with its first labor organizations and its first strike. That occurred in April, 1778, when the *Aufseher Collegium*, noting the fast depreciation of North Carolina paper money, ordered a general hike in price and wage levels. The Single Brothers, feeling that the rise was too little and too late, protested. When their protests were ignored they refused to work.

The strike was short lived. On April 11 the Single Brothers went back to work (without having gained their point) and, the *Collegium* reported, "the kiss of peace was given them."

Over the years, and almost imperceptibly, the socialistic controls in Salem relaxed a small bit at a time. But the lease system, the cornerstone of the Moravian system of community control, was not abandoned until November 11, 1856.

For 400 years these people stubbornly maintained their theocratic way of life within a larger society that was at first autocratic and, later, democratic. Besides offering a fine tribute to their skill at organization, that fact provides a measure of the zeal that sparked their Brotherhood.

Of all their traditions the Moravian love of music is, perhaps, the oldest and the deepest seated.

In 1501 the Brethren of Bohemia published the first Protestant Hymnal. From the very beginning these people enjoyed song and encouraged congregational singing.

Here, as in other areas, this small church has had a marked impact on Protestantism generally. Martin Luther, for example, lifted large chunks of the Moravian Hymnal of 1501. John Wesley, the founder of Methodism, translated many of the Moravian hymns from German into English and, in so doing, brought a new warmth into English hymn singing.

The classical period of music - the period of Haydn, Mozart and Beethoven - bracketed the years 1750-1800. Actually, however, the great works of those masters came within a limited period late in the century. But the groundwork for those few years was laid throughout the Eighteenth Century.

The Moravians came to America out of the heart of that period. Their musicians knew and worked with the leading musicians of that time. John Antes, a Moravian violinist and a composer, for example, knew Haydn and played in ensembles with him.

Music was as much a part of the Moravians' religious life as prayer.

Children entered life listening to the *Wiegenlieder* or cradle hymns. And the final notes of life were those of the trombones - the "last trumpet" in the "Going Home" of the Moravians - played from the belfry of the church.

In the morning and again in the evening Moravian families gathered about the table and recited "the daily words." They read the daily text, usually a Psalm, and then sang the words of the hymn dedicated to that particular day.

They sang as they worked. There were hymns for the sisters at their spinning wheels, for threshers and for those who plowed the fields. When the Moravians had "one for the road," they raised their voices (rather than cups) in *Reiselieder* or traveling hymns.

At harvest time men came into the fields with horns and oboes to play hymns of thanksgiving for the bounty of God. The love feasts were times of worship, fellowship and song.

In the Moravian towns there was music from dawn to dusk, and in the night the watchman made his rounds, blowing out blasts on his pierced conch, and chanting "The Song of the Hours."

This trait was unusual in Colonial America, for in the Eighteenth Century the Puritans and the stem doctrines of Calvinism frowned on almost all forms of musical expression. Where the Moravians used music to glorify God, the Puritans suspected that music - particularly instrumental music - was of the devil.

By 1746 the Moravians in Bethlehem were using an organ to accompany them in their singing. Most Moravian music called for instrumental accompaniment. These people were the first to bring instruments in any quantity and variety to America. They also were the first to use a variety of instruments in their church services.

They used trombones much as other churches used bells. Their trombone choirs (soprano, tenor, alto and bass) were unknown elsewhere in America. The choirs gathered to announce births, deaths, weddings, the arrival of distinguished guests, and all manner of community affairs.

The French horn was another favorite. In their churches men accompanied the singers on trumpets, flutes, bassoons, oboes, clarinets and even on the improbable zink.

The zink, a medieval trumpet with a mouthpiece of ox-horn, was last used in some of the compositions of Johann Sebastian Bach. Yet in 1805, at least a hundred years after the zink became extinct elsewhere, the Moravians in Salem ordered a pair specially made.

Along with the organ the Moravians in America used the piano, the harpsichord (a piano-like instrument in which strings are plucked by quills), the clavichord (here the strings are hammered with metal mallets), and the harp.

They were just as versatile when it came to stringed instruments, favoring the "fiholine," cello, and viola.

When the minister broke into song - and that he often did out of pure inspiration - the organist was expected to pick up the tune thread of the correct hymn (there were four hundred or so for the minister to choose from) and do that in precisely the correct key.

That sort of antiphonal music is a Moravian tradition, possibly dating back to the days when the church choir was separated, the men singing from one side of the communion table and the women from the other.

It helps explain how the massed bands at the Easter Sunrise Service will pick up a tune and then pass it back and forth, one band answering the other.

Musical skills run deep in these people. In most churches, for example, the congregation sings only the melody line while the choir tends to the harmony. Even today in a Moravian Church it isn't unusual to hear the entire congregation sing a hymn in well handled four-part harmony.

In Europe, during the time when music was largely limited to the church, institutions known as the *Collegia Musica* were formed. These were the symphony orchestras of the time and they brought music -most of it secular music - to the people.

A *Collegium Musicum* was established in Bethlehem before 1744. Salem organized its orchestra shortly after 1780.

Other cities - Philadelphia, Charleston, New York and Boston -had occasional concerts before 1740. But these were played by troupes of traveling musicians.

In the Moravian settlements these home-grown orchestras played regularly. The *Collegium Musicum* of Bethlehem probably was the first symphony orchestra in the United States (Charleston disputes that claim) while that in Salem was the third or fourth. And these early orchestras showed discernment in what they played. 'Haydn, for example, published his great oratorio, 'The Creation,' in 1800. It was played in Bethlehem in 1811 and, for the first time in the South, in Salem in 1829.

The curious thing about the musical tradition is that it existed in the absence of full-time professional musicians. The finest of the Moravian musicians were ministers and very busy men indeed.

Gottlieb Schober, for example, was an organist in Salem and the community's musical director. At one time or another in his busy life, Brother Shober was a weaver, tanner, schoolteacher, storekeeper, post-master, lawyer, and supervisor of the beggars who visited the village.

Christian Gregor (1723-1801) is known as the "father" of Moravian church music. When his other duties permitted, he would take the Daily Text and set it to music for voices and instrumental accompaniment. Thus he set a precedent for literally thousands of other Moravian compositions, both in Europe and in the American settlements.

Jeremiah Dencke (1725-1795) composed the first anthem known to have been written by Moravians in colonial America, a simple piece for chorus, strings, and organ for a provincial synod in Bethlehem in 1766. Of the many Moravian composers who served in America, Johann Friedrich Peter (1746-1813) was among the most talented and most prolific with over 80 works for voices and instrumental ensembles to his credit. His six string quintets may well be the first "classical" chamber works written in North America. He came to the new world with his brother Simon (also a gifted composer) in 1770 and served in Salem for ten years (1780-1790). While here he improved and expanded the community's *Collegium musicum*, composed a number of anthems, including one to celebrate the completion of the new church at Bethabara, and assembled the service for the first North Carolina celebration of Independence Day in 1783. His influence on musical life in Salem lasted long after he left in 1790 to serve congregations in Maryland, New Jersey, and Pennsylvania.

Moravian musicians, while they enjoyed playing instrumental music outside worship, preferred to devote their compositional talents to sacred vocal pieces. Their collection of instrumental music, purchased or copied from various sources, provides a wonderful cross-section of the musical tastes in late-eighteenth and early-nineteenth century Europe; many of these works are the only known surviving copies in the world.

During these years Moravians in both Europe and America composers were extremely active in composition. In Europe, for example, Johann Ludwig Freydt, John Antes, Johann Christian Geisler, and Christian Labtrobe, among many, worked in the circle surrounding Handel, Mozart, and Haydn. Latrobe and Antes, in particular, were acquainted with Haydn. Latrobe's three piano sonatas were published at Haydn's insistence and dedicated to him.

Composers working in America wrote in the classical tradition, starting from the same roots as their European brethren. However, since they were so isolated, compared to musicians in Herrnhut who had direct contact with contemporaries in Dresden, their works evolved more slowly. For example the works of J. L. Freydt, who was only two years younger than Peter, sound much more "romantic" than even Peter's late works.

As the nineteenth century moved on this heritage was affected in several ways in the new nation. First, more Moravians spoke English and fewer German and found what many editors and translators had long known: it is often much easier to write new music than it is to retain original elements in translation. Second, musical styles and tastes were changing; the classical style was yielding to a more romantic sound. Third, a whole new style of church music surrounded the Moravians in America-gospel hymns.

The Moravian tradition of writing music for specific needs did not end. Edward Leinbach (1823-1901), born and raised in Salem, was a capable composer who also taught at Salem Female Academy (later Salem Academy and College). Perhaps the most beloved of American Moravian tunes, especially among non-Moravians, is "Morning Star," written by Francis Florentine Hagen (1815-1907). While Hagen's own musical taste was somewhat trendy (he advocated the use of gospel hymns), his own compositions are marked by a straightforwardness which hearkens back to his classical Moravian roots while taking full advantage of the new "romantic" sound.

11

War - Revolutionary and Civil- And Change

The critical time for the Wachovia settlements came during the Revolutionary War period. For the Moravians the unrest of that period began early.

In 1765, when Great Britain imposed the Stamp Act, there was trouble in North Carolina. In part, the resentment of the King's Officers was not justified and consisted of little more than an objection to paying taxes to the Royal Governor or to anyone else.

But there was justification too. Residents of England could seize American property in Great Britain to satisfy debts. But when North Carolinians sought a reciprocal right the Royal Governor used his veto.

That typically arrogant attitude was deeply resented in the Colony.

By 1768 the Regulators were threatening to boot the Royal Officers right out of the Colony. In 1770 the Regulators became so bold the Governor called out the militia. Then, on May 16, 1771, Governor Tryon met the Regulators in Guilford County (the Battle of Alamance) and scattered them all the way to the Watauga settlements.

During this period the Moravians were in the embarrassing position of being suspected by both the Regulators and the King's men. The Salem diarist reported, "Our position brought us into danger that our houses and towns would be destroyed; even our lives were threatened, especially in May (1771), when threats were not only uttered here and there against us, but also came from the Government to whom false reports of us had been taken."

In all probability these false reports were the reason Governor Tryon marched his troops into the Wachovia towns immediately after the Battle of Alamance. He came there with three thousand men and remained for four days, accepting oaths of allegiance from former Regulators.

Tryon, who previously had respected the Moravians, quickly recognized that the reports he had been given about the treachery of the

Brethren and their disloyalty to the Crown were false. He had not been in Salem long before he lifted his glass in a happy toast "for the continued prosperity of the United Brethren in Wachovia."

But the suspicions of their neighbors did not abate. As war came closer - and, on April 19, 1775, broke into shooting at Lexington, Massachusetts - these suspicions hardened.

The Moravians were in an impossible position. They refused to take an oath of allegiance and they would not bear arms. More than that, they continued to pay rents on the Wachovia lands to the English even after others ignored all obligations to Britain.

They did their best to straddle this prickly fence. In 1775 they said". . . that they wished to remain true to the King; that they desired all good for the Province of North Carolina and would continue to do their best for it according to their ability." At about this same period they observed". . . we... live in the houses of peace."

But that was wishful thinking. When they supplied the Continental troops they aggravated the Loyalists. When they refused to shoulder arms, take an oath of allegiance, or openly denounce the King, their rebellious neighbors cocked their eyebrows and recalled that the peace-loving Brethren had shouldered guns during the time of the Indian Wars. From that bit of fact they jumped off to all types of unfounded rumors.

The Moravians, the Continentals said, had well-stocked stores because they continued to trade with the English. (So the Moravians, who stocked their stores from their own craft shops, reduced the goods displayed on their shelves.) It was reported that the Brethren had large supplies of powder and many guns hidden and that they secretly supplied the Indians with both. (The Moravians in this period took care not to display weapons and the little powder and lead they possessed were, indeed, well hidden.)

One of the touchy points was the new paper currency. The better class of people," the Moravians said, "had no fondness for it." That is understandable. By 1781 North Carolina paper money was worth one-eighth cent on the dollar.

The Moravians were reluctant to accept this money - some of them, like Brother Fockel, the storekeeper in Bethabara, actually refused to take it - but the law was plain. It said, "Who-so-ever will not accept it, or accepts it only at lower rates, or even speaks slightingly of it, shall be considered an enemy of the country."

The Moravians, making the unhappy best of a bad situation, re-luctantly accepted the paper money and then put it back into circulation with calculated, if unseemly, haste. Except, on occasion, to say that they had no change for so large a bill, the Moravians abided by the law.

As a result, they rarely saw hard money. Salem became the dumping place for the paper money. To make matters even worse, a goodly share of the money paid them was counterfeit.

But that was one of their lesser problems.

When the soldiers of Pulaski's Legion marched through Salem, they left smallpox behind them. Neighbors said they would burn Salem to the ground if the Moravians "spread the disease by inoculation." The result was forty-three cases of smallpox and three deaths.

As the war advanced, attempts were made to confiscate the Moravian lands. Under the law persons who refused to swear an oath of allegiance were considered Loyalists and their lands were taken from them.

On December 20, 1778, the Salem diarist reports, "Mr. Shepperd was here; the Senator hinted that our lands would be taken from us and that we would be driven away." Other men went beyond hints. They flatly said the Moravians were to lose their lands. Some of them went so far as to lay claims to certain of the Moravian towns.

But, once again, the passive resistance of the Brethren wore away hate. The one phrase in the oath of allegiance which offended the Moravians was amended and the Brethren were permitted to make an affirmation rather than swear an oath. That small bit of editing probably saved the Moravian towns.

Amidst all the scowls and threats there were occasional flashes of brutal violence. In 1779, for example, four men terrorized the village. They beat Brother George Frey until he was senseless and they knocked down Brother Heinzemann and then stomped, beat, gouged, and tomahawked him. There were cases where Brothers were stopped in the streets and had their coats stolen off their backs.

In 1780-81, as the center of the war swung into the South, conditions grew even worse.

First, Salem became a base for the Continental troops fighting Cornwallis in South Carolina. The prisoners taken at Kings Mountain were kept at Salem for a time and the village served as a powder depot and hospital for Continental troops.

As Cornwallis came north the American troops withdrew. But the militia, which was many times as dangerous, washed across Wachovia and those undisciplined men stole everything that wasn't nailed down or too heavy to carry. Their thefts ranged from the eggs taken from beneath a setting goose to livestock, potables, and the like.

On February 9, 1781, Cornwallis marched through Wachovia. Except for the camp followers (who stole the wash off the Single Brothers' line), his men maintained good order.

With Cornwallis gone the militia returned and threatened to burn the "Tory center." On February 17, Brother Bagge twice had a cocked pistol held at his chest while militia men mouthed threats.

After the British defeat at Guilford Courthouse on March 15, 1781, another wave of militia washed through the Moravian towns. For the Moravians, those from Wilkes County were the worst. "Some of them," the Moravians said, "were little better than bandits."

On July 4, 1783, the Moravians welcomed peace and the Psalm of the day was:

"Peace is with us! Peace is with us!

People of the Lord."

That day of celebration brought to an end a time which possesses a religious significance that deserves recognition. Here a handful of people - and in 1783 there were no more than a thousand Moravians in all of Wachovia - dared to be different, to refuse to bear arms, to refuse to take an oath, in a time when the land in which they lived was aflame with passion and filled with violence.

Others who did the same - the many thousands of Loyalists, for example - were uprooted and destroyed. Yet the Moravians escaped that fate though they had no protection stronger than their faith in the rightness of their way of life.

They genuinely believed that faith conquers all.

And so, in their case, it did.

The Moravians carried their distinctive customs and their rather aloof way of life into the Nineteenth Century. In 1801 they established a mission among the Cherokees and in 1838 that mission followed these tragic people down what they called "The Trail of Tears."

In 1822 the Sisters founded the "Salem Female Mission Society" and began to work more and more among the Negro slaves.

Originally the Moravians owned no slaves. As time went on they acquired a few. But, as Brother Marshall noted, "Not many of our Brothers and Sisters have the gift for handling slaves without spoiling them."

In their Sunday schools they taught reading and writing to the children of slaves even though this was contrary to the law of the state. In 1836 the Brethren held an unusual love feast in Salem in which they pledged their love to a party of Negroes who were leaving the United States to make homes for themselves in Liberia. Most of the members of that party died in Africa.

Throughout the years that preceded the Civil War there was political change. The Moravians purchased their land in what was then Anson County. When they built Bethabara they lived in Rowan County. They survived the Revolutionary War in Surry County and, shortly after the war ended, they were placed in Stokes. On January 1, 1849 Stokes was divided and the Wachovia lands became part of a new county called Forsyth.

That last change touched off an uproar in Salem. The conservative Brothers felt that a county seat was a home away from home for the devil. When Old Richmond was the county seat of Surry they said, "If you want to go to hell you need go no further than Richmond."

This conservative element wanted the county seat of Forsyth to be as far from Salem as was geographically possible. But there also was a younger group who said that the new town should be built directly to the north of Salem and that the streets of Salem should merely be continued to form the streets of the county seat.

Perhaps because Salem was located squarely in the center of the new county the progressives won that argument. On May 12, 1849, the Moravians sold fifty-one and a quarter acres of land for $256.25 as a site for the county town.

Until the new courthouse was completed the County Commissioners met in the Salem pottery. And for two years the new town itself was called Salem. But in January, 1851, the name was changed to Winston to honor Major Joseph Winston, a man from the Germanton area who served with distinction in the Revolutionary War. In 1913 this marriage of street patterns and convenience was formalized by a law which hyphenated the two towns.

These changes, brought on by the gradual and growing encroachment of the outside world on the Moravian towns, had their effect on the Moravians themselves and on their way of life.

During the 1850's the Salem diary shifted from German to English. The old lease system, the basis of the church control of the town, was abandoned. For the first time the Moravians broke completely free of the concept of the diaspora - the concept of the Brethren as a Christian way of life existing within other churches - and spoke of themselves as being members of a separate church.

In these same years many of the old ways were diluted to a point where they ceased to exist. The young men no longer refused to swear an oath and, as they proved in the Civil War, they abandoned their conscientious objections against bearing arms.

Of course, many of the traditional Moravian practices continued. The daily texts were read. The tradition of the love feasts continued and each Easter Morning the Brethren gathered in their God's Acre for the Sunrise Service.

The love for music continued, too. But the discriminating taste for fine music, perhaps because of the leveling influences coming in from the outside, all but disappeared except as it was preserved in the ancient hymnals. The *Collegium Musicum* gave way to the brass band. In very recent years that particular trend has reversed itself.

The Moravians did not stand apart during the bitter years of the Civil War. In June, 1861, three companies left Salem and marched off to war. There were Moravians in two of those companies and one of them, the Forsyth Rifles, was led by Captain A. H. Belo and outfitted by Francis Fries. Those Moravian boys fought and died on fields like Gettysburg right alongside other Tar Heel boys.

The Moravian towns were not hard hit by the war. Stoneman and his cavalry marched through Salem early in 1865 and, at the war's end, the Tenth Ohio Cavalry was stationed in the area.

In the Civil War and in the hungry, unhappy time of Reconstruction the Brethren shared the common lot of the people of this state. They no longer set themselves apart from all others in order jealously to preserve and protect their peculiar way of life.

In that change the Moravians themselves changed. But, while they came to adapt themselves to the ways of others, it also is true that they caused the imprint of their own character to be stamped on those who later came to live with them in their Wachovia towns. That fact - the fact of the lasting impact the Moravians have had upon our culture - brings us down to this day.

SUGGESTED READING

Fries, Adelaide L. The Road to Salem. Winston-Salem, John F. Blair, 1993

Gollin, Gillian Lindt. Moravians in Two Worlds. New York, Columbia University Press, 1967.

*Rauschenberg, Bradford. The Wachovia Historical Society,1895-1995. Wachovia Historical Society, 1995.

*Salem Remembrancers. Winston-Salem, Wachovia Historical Society, 1976.

Sensbach, Jon F. African-Americans in Salem, Winston-Salem, Old Salem, Inc., 1991.

A Separate Canaan: The Making of an Afro-Moravian World In North Carolina, 1763-1840. Chapel Hill, University of North Carolina Press, 1998.

Shirley, Michael. From Congregation Town to Industrial City. Culture and Social Change in a Southern Community. New York, New York University Press, 1999.

Smaby, Beverly Prior. The Transformation of Moravian Bethlehem. From Communal Mission to Family Economy. Philadelphia, University of Pennsylvania Press, 1988.

Sommer, Elisabeth W. Serving Two Masters: Moravian Brethren in Germany and North Carolina, 1727-1801.Lexington, University Press of Kentucky, 2000.

*South, Stanley. Historical Archeology in Wachovia. Excavating Eighteenth-Century Bethabara and Moravian Pottery. New York, Kluwer/Plenum, 1999.

Thorp, Daniel B. The Moravian Community in North Carolina: Pluralism on the Southern Frontier, Knoxville, University of Tennessee Press, 1989.

* Available from the Wachovia Historical Society.
    PO Box 106667
    Winston-Salem, NC 27108
    (336) 721-7373
    whsmail@earthlink.net
** Available from the Moravian Archives (Southern Province)
    4 East Bank Street
    Winston-Salem, NC 27101
    (336) 722-1742

MORAVIAN MUSIC TODAY

Much of what we know about the work of early American Moravian composers is because Moravians are "pack rats." With their longtime emphasis on education for all has come a sustained interest in their own history. During the earliest years of the Brethren in Bohemia and Moravia, they established the position of "archivist and writer," a person charged with preserving the Unity's important documents, writing its history, and interpreting its beliefs to others. This emphasis on preserving its heritage has given the Moravian Church a strength and deep-rootedness rare among American denominations. Such devotion to the treasures of the past is aptly demonstrated by the construction of the Archie K. Davis Center in Winston-Salem begun in 1999 to house both the Moravian Archives (Southern Province) and the Moravian Music Foundation.

Such respect for musical tradition leaves little doubt that Moravians will sing in the twenty-first and succeeding centuries just as they have in past and continue to hold music at heart of their individual and communal life.

For those interested in listening to Moravian music, Dr. Nola Reed Knouse, director of the Moravian Music Foundation, has compiled this list of easily available compact discs.

Lost Music of Early America – Music of the Moravians
Performed by the Boston Baroque, a period instrument ensemble with chorus, Martin Pearlman, Director. Telarc CD-80482

The Water Journey and Parthias 1 & 2 – David Moritz Michael (1741-1827) Performed by Pacific Classical Winds, a period instrument ensemble. New World Records 80490-2

By a Spring and Parthias 3, 4 & 5 – David Mortiz Michael (1751-1827) Performed by Pacific Classical Winds, a period instrument ensemble New World Records 80531-2

David Moritz Michael: Parthias 6-9: This continues the series of Michael wind music recorded by Pacific Classical Winds and produced by New World Records. As you listen through all of the parthien thus far released, you can trace the development of Michael's compositional technique – his writing becomes more sophisticated and more intriguing. Once again, the performance and the recording quality are wonderful! New World Records #80538-2.

__Three String Trios__ – John Antes (1740-1811) & Six String Quintets – Johann Friedrich Peter (1746-1813) performed by American Moravian Chamber Ensemble, a period insturment ensemble.
New World Records 80507-2 (double CD set)

__A Psalm of Joy__ – Johann Friedrich Peter (1746-1813)
Music of the First Fourth of July Celebration, Held in Salem, NC,
July 4, 1783. Available through the Moravian Music Foundation office.

__Music for All Seasons: Moravian Trombones: Chorales,   Sonatas, Occasional   Music__ - Performed   by   the   Los   Angeles   Philharmonic Trombone Ensemble and the Moravian Trombone Choir of Downey.
Crystal Records CD 220

INDEX

For Reference

Not to be taken from this room